TO STOP A RISING SUN

REMINISCENCES OF WARTIME IN INDIA AND BURMA

Roy Humphreys

with a foreword by

The Countess

Mountbatten of Burma

ALAN SUTTON PUBLISHING LIMITED

First published in the United Kingdom in 1996
Alan Sutton Publishing Limited
Phoenix Mill · Far Thrupp · Stroud · Gloucestershire

British Library Cataloguing in Publication Data
A catalogue record for this book is available from the British Library

ISBN 0-7509-1181-6

Typeset in 11/13 Bembo.
Typesetting and origination by
Alan Sutton Publishing Limited.
Printed in Great Britain by
Butler & Tanner, Frome, Somerset.

Contents

History with its flickering lamp stumbles along the trail of the past, trying to reconstruct its scenes, to revive its echoes, and rekindle with pale gleams the passion of former years.

Winston S. Churchill

Foreword

As Vice Patron of the Burma Star Association I am especially pleased that Roy Humphreys has gathered together this moving collection of wartime reminiscences of some of my father's Burma Stars.

Although over half a century has passed since that terrible jungle warfare these memories will always remain fresh for the men who took part, and serve to record for the next and future generations a vivid picture of the conditions in which their fathers and grandfathers had to live, and survive, let alone fight. Our admiration for those heroes is unbounded, and for the amazing fighting spirit which kept them going till victory was achieved.

My father, as Supreme Allied Commander in South East Asia, had the highest admiration, as well as real affection, for all the men who served with him. Reading these reminiscences – tragic, brave, sad, laced with well-timed moans and humour – gives a picture of what war is really like 'at the sharp end', that no accounts from senior officers, concerned, as they are mainly with strategy and interesting as they may be to read, can ever give.

I share my father's feelings for those who served with him and feel very proud that my husband (Lord Brabourne, who was his ADC) and I are also Burma Stars and know the background well.

Mountbatten of Burma

THE COUNTESS MOUNTBATTEN OF BURMA

Acknowledgements

Much of the appeal of this book, is to pick out strands of interwoven thought, feeling and action. All of the contributors are individuals – each different from the next, among them many unsung heroes, who weave a tapestry of experience second to none. I acknowledge with sincere gratitude the contributions made by the following.

R. Temblett; A. Newman; D. Wood; K. Flint; Lieutenant Colonel A. A. Mains; W. Johnson; G. Swinney; R. Dunne; Squadron Leader R. T. D. Smith AFM; R. Spencer; H. Suttie; Major S. Hamilton MBE; P. Cummins; B. Lamb; H. Eyley; G. Liddell; R. Todd; L. Thomas; V. Gregory; W. Savage; L. Powell; C. Edwards; C. Buckthorpe; A. Turner; P. Mortakis; P. James; J. H. Chew; Lieutenant Colonel C. D. Christmas; M. Nash; A. Tiller; Helen Price; R. Holland; M. Nash; M. McCoy-Hill; H. Russell; A. Driver; J. Smith; J. F. Warren; Captain E. C. Hamlyn; G. Warrener; E. Poole; R. T. Davis; Dr R. G. Miller, MA, MD FRCP; R. Foster; E. R. Parsons; Major J. Shave; J. White; A. Dickson; R. Wintle; P. Chapman; Revd J. Marshall MA; Lieutenant Colonel C. D. C. Frith OBE; K. Short; R. Millward; Captain D. A. T. Thain; D. Cobb; D. Moore; F. Stone; C. Owen; A. J. Humphreys; R. Demmery; F. Booton; A. Griffiths; M. W. Swinhoe-Phelan; T. Brookes; Kitty Jones; T. E. White CGM; J. Bamford; R. Child; L. Atkinson; E. Horner; Helen Hughes; W. Parker; K. Orton; P. James; C. Tilley; F. Browne; W. Barnard; D. Wright; Catherine Cleary; H. E. Bowles; J. R. Allan; L. Upcott; S. Eadon; C. Bissler; W. Adams; T. W. McKie; R. Leagas; W. H. Davies; Kay Smith; R. Mathews; S. Morley; W. A. Millward.

Preface

Fifty years on from the happenings of war, a time of drama and dreadful experience before the eyes of all the world, the recollections of feats of arms are beginning to fade. The theatre of war was so vast, its geography beyond the concept of the ordinary soldier, sailor or airman.

Within the pages of books about the last war few, if any, record the actual impressions of experience. As for the 14th Army – dubbed by the National newspapers as the 'Forgotten Army' – it was their avowed intention to get back on the offensive and to drive out the Imperial Japanese forces from the borders of India.

This book records the experiences of the ordinary men and women who were thrust into uniform and found themselves in a strange, and sometimes hostile country – a country about which few had any conclusive knowledge. The collection of reminiscences are essentially their own, and reveal how they saw their experience. In spite of the many uncertainties of war they made the best of it. Laughing and joking, they may have been in their usual inimitable and time-honoured fashion, often voicing their pungent statements to colonels and staff alike, but they were admirable in battle.

There are times when one wonders if the war record of a nation at arms will ever be of the slightest interest to the modern generation. To put the record straight, however, I feel incumbent to set down these experiences of things past while they are still fresh in the mind. Much of our knowledge of former times we owe to the writings of those who served in the humbler ranks.

Seeing archive film of the Burma war during the 50th anniversary of VJ Day, one felt nothing but sorrow. Before one's eyes the by now familiar images on the television screen revealed the young men tramping through jungles and muddy rivers, the ruins of villages, towns and cities, and the unforgettable skeletal figures of the POWs. There was a plethora of mixed emotions – sombre and complicated; awestruck admiration for the courage of the 14th Army and especially the Chindits, stomach-turning sympathy for their sufferings, disgust at the cruelty and carnage, the certain grief for their comrades who died in Battles, alone in ditches or field dressing stations as a result of wounds or tropical diseases.

One could not help the rush of feeling of such analloyed admiration for the men who endured extraordinary drama, pain and heroism. I doubt if any old soldier could pretend to have any generous feeling towards the Japanese, whose debased cruelty towards thousands was so unnecessary.

Roughly 53,096 Allied troops perished in the Burma campaign, all are commemorated on memorials and include the unidentified. The numbers listed as missing and who have no known grave, lie somewhere in that vast area of jungle and the inaccessible mountain terrain. The macabre and grotesque, scattered across the rich soil of Burma, gave their bodies to the cause of freedom – their souls to God.

This was fighting such as few soldiers in the European theatre of war had endured.

The regulation Wolseley Helmet, proudly worn by these RAF newcomers to India, was soon replaced by the bush hat.

Glossary and Abbreviations

There are several hundred dialects and several main languages in the sub-continent of India but the lingua franca of the Indian Army is Urdu. British troops who had daily dealings with Indians would have had a working knowledge of Urdu, which they preferred to call Hindustani. The following covers most of the working, everyday language.

accha	good	jao	go
asti	slowly	jildi	quickly
badmash	undesirable	karo	do
bahut	very	khud	hillside
baksheesh	tip, alms or gift	kiswaste	why
bas	enough	kya	what
basha	native hut	lathi	stave
bhisti	water carrier	maidan	open ground
bibi	girl	mallum	understand
burra	big	mukkin	butter
chaggal	canvas water bag	nappi	barber
chapal	sandals	nichi	underneath
char	tea	pani	water
charbash	well done	pialla	enamelled mug
charpoy	rope bed	pice	small coin
chatti	earthenware jug	puggle-pani	alcoholic drink
chaung	dry river bed	pukka	genuine
chota	small	sahib	sir or mister
coggage	paper	salaams	greetings
dacoit	robber	sepoy	soldier
daftar	office	shikari	hunter
dekko	look	susti	lazy
dhobi	laundry	tiffin	midday meal
durri	coarse woven rug	tonga	one horse cart
eepyipi	army tent	upper	above
ek	figure 1	wallah	servant
hogiya	finish	yakdan	leather pannier
idhar-ao	come here		

Indian Army Ranks

Subedar Major	Senior Viceroy's Commissioned Officer, Major	Jemadar	VCO Lieutenant
		Havildar	Sergeant
		Naik	Corporal
Subedar	VCO Captain	Lance Naik	Lance Corporal

Admin Box	Maintenance area	NCO	Non Commissioned Officer
AFS	American Field Service	NES	No Enemy Seen
AIR	All-India Radio	NWF	North West Frontier
BGH	British General Hospital	OP	Observation Post
BMH	British Military Hospital	QAIMNS	Queen Alexandra's Imperial
BOR	British Other Rank		Military Nursing Service
CCS	Casualty Clearing Station	QM	Quartermaster
CGM	Conspicuous Gallantry Medal	RA	Royal Artillery
CO	Commanding Officer	RAMC	Royal Army Medical Corps
CQMS	Company Quarter Master	RAOC	Royal Army Ordnance Corps
	Sergeant	RAP	Regimental Aid Post
CSM	Company Sergeant Major	RAPWI	Repatriation Allied Prisoners
EA	East African		of War and Internees
ENSA	Entertainments National	RASC	Royal Army Service Corps
	Services Association	RE	Royal Engineers
FOO	Forward Observation Officer	REME	Royal Electrical Mechanical
FSO	Field Service Officer		Engineers
GHQ	General Head Quarters	RHQ	Regimental Head Quarters
GOC	General Officer Commanding	RIASC	Royal Indian Army Service
HAA	Heavy Ack Ack		Corps
HMIS	His Majesty's Indian Ship	RIN	Royal Indian Navy
HQ	Headquarters	RSM	Regimental Sergeant Major
IGH	Indian General Hospital	RTO	Railway Transport Officer
IOR	Indian Other Rank	SEAC	South East Asia Command
KOYLI	Kings Own Yorkshire Light	TCP	Traffic Control Post
	Infantry	VAD	Voluntary Aid Detachment
LAD		VCO	Viceroy Commissioned
LCT	Landing Craft Tank		Officer
LMG	Light Machine Gun	WA	West African
MAS	Medical Aid Station	WAAC	Women's Army Auxiliary
MDS	Medical Dressing Station		Corps
MO	Medical Officer	WAAF	Women's Auxiliary Air Force
MT	Motor Transport	WRNS	Women's Royal Naval Service

CHAPTER ONE

'No Kill Snake, Sahib!'

Below the general, below the staff, there were above all the soldiers. In this theatre of war the various campaigns gathered together, like a whirlpool, men from the ends of the earth. There were English, Irish, Welsh and Scots, and in the RAF there were Newfoundlanders, Australians, Canadians, New Zealanders and South Africans. There were the Chinese; there were tall slender Negroes from East Africa and darker, more heavily built Negroes from West Africa, with the tribal slits cut deep into their cheeks – an infantry division of each.

There were also the Chins, Kachines, Karens and Burmese, mostly light brown, small-boned men in worn jungle green, doubly heroic because the Japanese held possession of their homes, often of their families too, and they were unsure which side was going to win.

American C47s making a supply drop over Burma. 'Other Dakotas were passing us on their way back to base, having dropped their supplies to the Chindits.'

Lastly and in by far the greatest numbers, there were the men of the Indian Army – the largest volunteer army the world has ever known; men from every caste and race. There were the Sikhs, Dogras, Pathans, Madrassis, Rajputes, Assamese, Kumaonis, Punjabis, Garhwalis, Naga head hunters and, from Nepal, the Gurkhas in all their tribes and sub-tribes, of Limbu and Rai, Thapa and Chhetri, Magar and Gurung. These men wore turbans and steel helmets and slouch hats and berets and tank helmets and khaki shakoes – the latter inherited from the eighteenth century. There were Americans, too.

There were companies that averaged 5 feet 1 inch in height and others that averaged 6 feet 1 inch. There were men as purple-black as the West Africans and men as pale of skin as golden wheat, like a lightly sun-tanned blonde. They worshipped God according to the rites of the Mahayana and Hinayana, of Sunni and of Shia, of Rome and Canterbury and Geneva, of Vedas and the sages and the Mahabharatas, of the guru, of the secret shrines of the jungle.

There were vegetarians, meat-eaters and fish-eaters; men who only ate rice, and men who only ate wheat, men who had four wives, men who shared one wife with four brothers and men who openly practised sodomy. There were men who had never seen snow and men who seldom saw anything else, and there were Brahmins and the Untouchables – both with rifle and Tommy gun.

Soldiers of the Indian Airborne stand in sombre silence beside the bodies of their enemy – an enemy often described as undefeatable.

No one who saw the 14th Army in action, above all no one who saw its dead on the field of battle – the Black and White and the Brown and the Yellow lying together in their indistinguishable blood on the rich soil of Burma – can ever doubt that there is a brotherhood of man.

Unless you have experienced the trauma of jungle warfare it is quite impossible to describe the conditions under which the men of the 14th Army fought at that time. Always under fire and frequently without adequate supplies, they faced a ruthless enemy who had often been regarded as undefeatable. The courage of the Allied servicemen and women in Burma and India has become a legend, and their final victory regarded as one of the greatest in the history of warfare. To be seriously wounded in the heat of battle was only the beginning of a terrible ordeal. Thousands of Allied soldiers injured in front-line positions died before they could receive urgent medical attention. The lucky ones ended up at one of the base general hospitals in India.

FEVER SONG

An original poem contributed by ex-QAIMNS Kitty Jones.

> And did you serve in India, lad,
> Or Burma's wild green land?
> And did you have the fever there
> Till you could scarcely stand?
> And does the fever catch you still
> When England's winds blow bitter chill?
>
> And does your head throb once again
> As it did then, my lad?
> And do you feel the dulling pain
> The same as you once had?
> And do you, soldier, curse the day
> When under those hot skies you lay?
>
> And do you shake and shiver, lad,
> And ache to lay you down,
> As you did then, short years ago,
> Under the jungle's crown?
> And do you sigh for water now,
> And drink the salt sweat from your brow?

And do your limbs feel far away
In ague's sudden grip?
And do you like the price you pay,
The fever-cup you sip,
For being young in England's Isle
When Hitler saw his war-god smile?

Or do you think of well-known friends,
Men of your Company,
Who, uncomplaining, met their ends,
Nor looked for sympathy;
But under Asia's brassy skies
Died with this England in their eyes?

Their rotted bones in jungle lie
Six thousand miles away –
Lad, what's a fever? You won't die.
You'll live another day –
But God forgive, if you forget
They paid, in agony, our debt.

'Their rotted bones in jungle lie six thousand miles away –'
The first Kohima cemetery showing the Naga rock in the distance.

R. Temblett
SOMERSET LIGHT INFANTRY

We left Blighty in November 1939 and on arrival in India went to the Punjab, where we began a recruiting march from Multan across the Chenab River to Dehra, a round journey of over 200 miles. We enlisted about a dozen recruits but half of them deserted at night taking their kit and uniform with them. Luckily at this stage they had not been issued with rifles.

After being stationed in Delhi, Lahore and Calcutta, where I saw the fabulous Taj Mahal, we were posted to the constant trouble spots of the North West Frontier. Luckily I was not attacked by screaming tribesmen carrying 2 foot long Afghan knives, or picked off by Pathan snipers hiding in ambush. In fact, what sticks in my mind most of all was being cut off by floods of all things, and having to be supplied by camels in convoy.

Then on to Burma driving a Bren gun carrier over the Mayey range of mountains by way of the Nichedaw Pass. It was a treacherous route with huge ravines. Our strict orders were that if a vehicle broke down there was to be no time wasted trying to repair it. We pushed them down the khuds. The pass was a graveyard of abandoned vehicles. How we survived in the Admin Box I will never know. Three hardtack biscuits and a bottle of water were often the day's ration. 'Johnny Gurkha' was a great bloke to soldiers alongside him. He possessed a real sense of humour. I once saw a Jap's head by the trackside with a smouldering cigarette in its mouth and a hand sticking out of the soil as if it was going to take it out. Another time I saw a dead mule lying by the roadside with two mule drivers crying and wailing beside it. A British padre came along and tried to comfort them. He remarked that he was happy to see they had sympathy for one of God's creatures. They were quick to reply – in their own tongue – that they had no sympathy for the blessed creature and were actually complaining to anyone who would listen that they had to bury the wretched animal.

Back to the North West Frontier. It was still fairly quiet, although there was the occasional tribal incident so we had to be constantly on our guard. I remember there was a bazaar there called the 'Lus Wallahs Bazaar', a sort of thieves' market where all kinds of valuables like silk and ivory could be purchased.

I was eventually roped in for another recruiting drive but this time in vehicles. I drove from Peshawar down to Quetta, and then through the Sind Desert to Karachi, with an oldish Sikh sepoy as my co-driver. At one stage we both fell asleep through exhaustion and heat with the result that we drove straight into a large rock head-on.

'Back to the North West Frontier. It was still fairly quiet, although there was the occasional tribal incident.'

A.J. Humphreys
ROYAL WEST AFRICAN FRONTIER FORCE

Most of the troops who left the UK with me in 1941 were destined for India. I had been posted to an HAA Battery and went with them to Freetown, West Africa. Within a short time the unit of 372 was whittled down to 89 and integrated with other ranks from Nigeria, into the 2nd (WA) HAA Regiment, part of the Royal West African Frontier Force.

We had to change ships in Cape Town and there was some difficulty accommodating us on other, fully loaded ships for the last part of the journey. However, room could be found in a troopship that was just docking at Durban on the other side of the continent.

The decision was made. We would travel across southern Africa by train. Not just an ordinary train, like those in the UK, with junior ranks pushed into overcrowded third-class carriages, but one of their luxury transcontinental trains with all the usual extras. Each compartment seated six very comfortably and our meals were served, along the corridor, in one of the dining cars. The train had a lounge with a bar and we could relax there while black attendants converted our compartment into a six-berth sleeping quarter. When we returned we found the beds made up, three on each side, one above the other. The central table had been stored away, to reveal a hand basin for washing with hot and cold water, clean towels and a small bar of soap.

The two engines, good old-fashioned steam locomotives, left the main station at Cape Town and, with the usual toot on the whistle, moved slowly inland. Passing Table Mountain, we climbed from sea level to the plateau, some 3,000 feet above. That part of the trip took about twelve hours and the track changed direction continuously to avoid high peaks.

The lush green of the coastal region soon changed to a dusty brown colour and the almost desert-like appearance of the landscape continued for most of the journey. We passed through Kimberley and Johannesburg before turning south for Durban. The train passed quickly through Ladysmith, once a town under seige during the Boer War, and stopped a while at Pietermaritzburg where our steam engine was replaced by an electric one for the last part of the journey. During the forty-eight hours we were aboard, the train covered some 1,400 miles at an average speed of 30 miles an hour. We had enjoyed three square meals each day, played cards and viewed a part of the world that few British soldiers had had the opportunity of seeing.

The coaches were shunted to the dockside and we walked straight from the train to the troopship which was tied alongside. The ship's departure had been delayed for us and almost as soon as we had boarded, tugs began moving the liner away from her berth and towards the open sea. It was approaching dusk as we edged our way out of the docks and I was one of the passengers lining the rails ready to bid farewell to South Africa.

Below, on the jetty, we saw a lone figure whom I now know to have been a certain Mrs Gibson. In fair weather or foul, she would stand on the point at Durban and sing to all the troops as they entered harbour or left on their journey.

Perla Siedle Gibson, a professional concert soprano, sang her favourite piece 'Land of Hope and Glory', until her voice failed to reach us, although we could still see her standing on the wharf. After the war Mrs Gibson was instrumental in raising funds from the people of Natal Province, which was her way of saying thank you to the Allied Forces for their sacrifice in defence of freedom. Mrs Gibson died in 1971 and a bronze statue, *The Lady in White*, designed and cast by her niece, Barbara Siedle, was erected at Durban's T-jetty in August 1995.

During the Second World War more than 400 convoys, 45,000 ships and 6 million service personnel passed through South African ports en route to and from Mediterranean and Far Eastern war zones. Over half of them stopped at Durban, and few will have forgotten its legendary 'Lady in White'.

'Below, on the jetty, we saw a lone figure whom I now know to have been a certain Mrs Gibson. In fair weather or foul, she would stand on the point at Durban and sing to all the troops . . .'

IF WE HAD NEVER MET

If we had never met,
How oft I ponder thinking thus,
And go my thoughts as in a game,
Through 'ifs' and 'buts' and back again,
Returning in all truthfulness
To tell me this,
How empty life had been for us,
If we had never met.

If you had never cared,
I should have passed all beauty by;
Unheeding at the dawn, the flame,
That puts the murky night in shame;

Perla Siedle Gibson, known to thousands of servicemen as 'The Lady in White', sang her favourite piece 'Land of Hope and Glory', 'until her voice failed to reach us . . .'.

The loveliness of eventide
I had not shared,
For love this lonely heart had died,
If you had never cared.

R.H.P.
26 May 1945

Arthur Newman
CORPS OF MILITARY POLICE

My most memorable experience is also the most shocking. During an outbreak of cholera we had to mount a patrol between Kalyan Camp and Bombay. Two of the patrol had disappeared and I set out with two other military policemen to a village where we suspected they might have gone.

It was a sight I shall never forget – the sick, the dying and the dead. Without medical training there was nothing we could do, and as soon as we three had located the missing pair we left that village just as fast as we could. Luckily, we had all just been inoculated against cholera but that did not make us any the less frightened of this terrible disease.

D. Wood
16 PARA BATTALION

'Lakri' Lowrie woke the whole basha up one night shrieking that he was being attacked by snakes. When we finally got him calmed down we found he had been wrestling with the webbing straps on his large pack. A few nights later the platoon spent the night in the jungle hunting for a tiger. They had heard a noise in the dense undergrowth (probably made by a troop of baboons). In the event, they let fly with a fusillade from their No. 5 jungle rifles in all directions for about ten minutes. In the morning there was nothing to be seen except for a few trees with bullet-ridden trunks!

We had one chap who used to sneak craftily off to an Indian village to buy palm toddy, which is fiery stuff to drink at any time. We were doing an exercise in Kaki Kalam and it was sweltering hot. Instead of filling his water bottle with water he poured in the native spirit. He kept taking swigs during the exercise because he needed something to keep him going. But he finished up going back to camp on a jeep stretcher, well strapped in, and singing at the top of his voice, 'I love a lassie – a black Madrassi lassie . . .'. The rest of his rendition is not repeatable.

Lieutenant Colonel A.A. Mains
9TH GURKHA RIFLES

I arrived in Rangoon the very day of the Japanese invasion. My task was to raise 4 Security Section. There were available armed police, a sort of para-military Burma Military Police consisting of mostly Karens and other tribal personnel plus Gurkhas, Garwhalis, Kumaonis, Sikhs and Punjabi Musselmans, and ordinary unarmed civil police drawn mainly from Burmans.

About the time the Japanese started to bomb Rangoon there was a staggering number of police desertions. They just seemed to melt away as the war situation intensified in their particular area. When the time came to evacuate Rangoon, I had retained in the city the nucleus of a field security section, made up of one officer, a VCO and six IORs, augmented by a further six BORs, all from the Gloucesters.

About 22 February 1942, I was ordered to take the section to Rangoon railway station and place it under the command of a colonel Deputy Director of Railways. We were to keep order at the station, oversee the orderly loading of trains and protect railway staff from any assault. The Rangoon civil police should have been doing this duty but were making little effort.

The policy at that time was not even to attempt to hold Rangoon. The 'privileged' from hospitals and communications and municipal employees had been promised evacuation if they remained at their posts until the last minute, before being sent to comparative safety in Mandalay. On the second day I was told that some two hundred Rangoon police were demanding immediate transport to Mandalay. They were threatening to storm the railway station. All I could do was to deploy my tiny 'army' of fourteen men and be ready to open fire if the police mob tried to break through the barrier. Fortunately, the Deputy Commissioner of Police arrived and it transpired they should have been told they were to board a train for Prome – not Mandalay.

Meanwhile the police had been systematically looting the cloth bazaar. The rule, however, was one package per man, so my section had to divest them of their ill-gotten gains and some of the mob received a whack from my men's lathis in the process. But at this stage in the proceedings the Deputy Commissioner of Police turned up. The result was a verbal set-to!

When the station job was over I was told that new orders from Winston Churchill, the Prime Minister, had decreed Rangoon would be held. An Australian division, on their way home by sea, would be diverted to the city and also an augmented Indian infantry division would arrive. I was then appointed Assistant Military Governor with more or less full powers over law and order. British civilians were carrying out essential work at the docks and my job was to make it safe for them to move about.

There were no magistrates, and inmates of jails, lunatic asylums and even animals from the zoo roamed freely, and with hardly any police to speak of, the situation became impossible. But the police who were available, both officers and sergeants, seemed willing enough to take orders from me, despite the fact that on record I was singularly referred to as 'quite ruthless'. Between us and some garrison military police we managed to keep order in the centre of Rangoon until the final evacuation, but not without a certain amount of firearm use! The police escaped by sea but because of the shortage of space the army personnel came out by road with the rear guard of the Gloucesters, narrowly escaping capture at Taukkyan Bend.

W. Johnson
ROYAL ARTILLERY

I joined as a regular gunner in May 1939 and my sweetheart, Florence, came to see me off from Woolwich railway station. Her parting words were, 'Will you write to me?' I did, and we married in March 1941. By September I was on embarkation leave and it was October 1945 before I was home again. The army kept me hanging about before sending me back to India, where I shuttled back and forth between Delhi, Deolali and Poona, before sailing from Bombay in June 1942.

Part of the Tiddim Road in Burma was called the Chocolate Stairway because of the colour of the naked earth. It rose to over 3,000 feet through 7 miles of hair-pin bends on a gradient of 1 in 12. Mules, men and vehicles trampled it into ankle-deep mud. During the almost continuous wet season, huge sections of the road would often suddenly disappear in a thunderous landslide.

I hated the soya-link sausages; they were unappetizing, unfriable and jolly near uneatable too. How we existed I really don't know. Nobody had any spare fat on him. But the rum ration was always generous and cigarettes were plentiful, often sent out to us by well-wishers at home, and some from private schools in the south of England.

Monsoons were dreadful. Mountains were continually shrouded in wet mists and then the clouds would come racing in. This would go on for over three weeks at a time with no let up. Then came the violent thunderstorms when visibility was down to nil. Clothing, bedding, accommodation all became very damp with no chance of drying out. Food, if a fire could be kept going, tasted musty, cigarettes became soggy and tended to disintegrate, stamps and envelopes simply stuck together and footwear developed a thick mildew. And since there was hardly a metalled road in any operational area, the dirt roads deteriorated into tracks that even a bullock cart could barely negotiate. The heat was insufferable. But God's handwriting was everywhere – the sound of the coppersmith bird with its endless 'knocking' call, the 'tuck too' of the lizard, the absolute silence at sundown and the jungle grasses whispering in the early wind of dawn. It may sound like sentimentality, but although it was a hard and dangerous life, and I did not want to die, those raw experiences I endured now have a value worth more than all the gold in the Rand mines.

I don't think we felt any great hatred towards the Japanese, and I suppose, looking back on it all, indifference sums up what most of us felt. After all, they are a race cast in a different mould. I cannot ever forget what they did and neither do I go along with forgiveness – noble as that might be.

Christmas 1942 was spent on the Imphal–Palel Road, squatting in the shadow of the jungle undergrowth, Tommy gun cradled across the left arm, eyes trying to pierce the darkness of the night, watching for the slightest movement on the track ahead. Part of one's mind inevitably drifted back to Blighty, across thousands of miles. In my mind's eye I could see the scene at home, a roaring fire in the grate, the crisp, white cloth on the table, the family, including my wife and our little daughter, seated around the laden table eating and chatting.

This vision of home helped to sustain me. I can remember looking at the huge golden Burma moon and thinking that it was the same moon that shone

'I would close my eyes for a second, kiss the butt of my rifle and trust in God to see me through.'

on Blighty. I would close my eyes for a second, kiss the butt of my rifle and trust in God to see me through. To see this great golden moon, hanging like some sacred oriental gong surrounded by thousands of twinkling stars, used to fill me with a sense of longing.

One date, 6 June 1944, just four days before my twenty-fourth birthday, stands out in my mind. I had been three years in Burma – a land full of exciting place-names, names that turned out to be a disappointment: Shwebo, Sangshak, Imphal, Tamu Kalewa and Palel – some of them not even villages, let alone towns. Just a scattering of bashas, often burned to the ground like Shenam. The hills, rising to over 5,000 feet, were either occupied by the Japanese troops or overlooked by them. If you moved, it was always at the double, for fear of being shot by a sniper. On 6 June I was trying to sew a button on my trousers. Down the hillside came the familiar figure of our captain together with two of our wireless operators. I watched their slow progress through the steaming jungle then heard the captain's voice: 'Cheer up, chaps – cheer up, they have just made a landing in Normandy. They really have started the Second Front at last!' It was wonderful news, but would it take some of the load off our shoulders?

George Swinney
'S' COMPANY 2ND BATTALION BLACK WATCH

George Swinney and the rest of his draft had struggled down the gangway of the troopship at Bombay, through the dockside sheds, where they retrieved their kit bags, and were packed into a trooptrain by the friendly squaddies of the transport staff.

It was all very strange, the smell of India a contrast to the shipboard smells they had endured for the past five weeks. As soon as they were packed into the train the hawkers quickly appeared with their fruit, brass rings that were 'genuine gold', watches and everything else they thought would sell. The squaddies had been issued with five rupees on disembarking but as they had no true measure of the value of this currency, they did not indulge in a spending spree; most of them had the essential ration of cigarettes and next to that the only item of importance was food.

As the train began to wend its way through the Indian countryside most of the squaddies lapsed into a contemplative silence as they surveyed first the sights of urban Bombay's packed humanity, then the bullocks in the paddy fields, with a raucous shout for the occasional bibis in their bright, colourful saris.

No one had bothered to tell them where they were going, so they did what soldiers always do, settled down as comfortably as the wooden seats would allow, and went to sleep. It was hot but no worse than the crowded troop decks had been. They had no sooner settled when the train stopped at a small wayside station. Someone – bless him! – had decided it was time they were introduced to India's most famous institution, the char-wallah. There were dozens of these individuals lining the station platform and as soon as the train had stopped, each char-wallah selected a carriage and climbed aboard.

'Char-wallah sahib, char-wallah,' the very first words of Urdu that every British soldier was to learn, followed by 'Egg banjo, sahib'. These sturdy vendors of that essential brew and its accompaniment, tea and egg rolls, worked their way down the carriage. There was no need to haggle over the price, that was fixed at a sacrosanct four annas, now and forever.

Strangely enough it was from the char-wallah that they discovered that their destination was to be Kalyan Camp. The char-wallahs always knew these things, even before the sergeants did!

Kalyan Camp was about 2 miles from the infamous Deolali Camp, the latter better known for the service derivation 'Doolally Tap' meaning 'going daft' – 'tap' being Urdu for fever. Kalyan was in fact a holding camp for troops where you might spend three weeks before being posted to your unit. These three weeks gave the soldiers a little time to get used to the country, its climate and all the other annoyances they would be required to tolerate. They disembarked from the train, were formed into squads and then marched into Kalyan. George and his squad found themselves allocated to an empty patch of hard-packed mud between some wooden huts. A strange sergeant appeared and ordered them to leave their kit on the ground then marched them off to the stores to draw mosquito nets and chaggals, green coloured uniforms, new boots and puttees and wide baggy shorts.

They were inoculated, vaccinated and issued with mosquito repellent cream, herded into a mess hall and had their first meal in India, with instructions to empty their slops into the buckets outside. George was by this time totally lacking in appetite and did not enjoy his food. Taking his mug of char he decided that a quiet smoke outside would be more beneficial. Mug in one hand and his plate of uneaten food in the other, he walked towards the slop bins. Suddenly a large bird swooped down, grabbed the meat from his plate and, with a loud cry of triumph, soared skywards. George had met his first 'Shite Hawk' – the indigenous kite hawk of India, a bird named for its preference for British Army food, a sure sign of insanity in any animal or soldier. Never again would George approach a swill bin with an uncovered plate.

Back at the space where they had left their kit, the sergeant appeared with the bad news. 'The draft that was due to go this afternoon is not going until tomorrow. Their hut is not available so you will have to bed down where you are for the night. Spread your groundsheets, prop up the end of your mosquito net with a stick and tuck the edges under your groundsheet. You'll be OK.' With that he disappeared to the place where sergeants go, which is not always the place BORs would wish.

George settled down for the night as per instructions; at this point in his army life he was at best a soldier aspiring to the rank of lance corporal.

They were beside a native cookhouse of some kind and the chatter of the cooks was the background music that made him drift off to sleep. George tossed and turned on the hard ground consoled by the thought that tomorrow he would at least have a bed. But the noise from the cookhouse slowly brought George out of his uncomfortable sleep. He felt for the edge of the mosquito net to pull it clear from the groundsheet and became aware of a large lump under the sheet. Finally managing to free himself, he pulled the groundsheet clear to see what the lump was. George was not a snake lover and there, curled up under his groundsheet, was the biggest snake he had ever seen.

His startled yell caused several of the native cooks to run out in alarm. One of them reached out and grabbed the still dozing snake by the head saying, 'No kill snake, sahib', then ran off with it. 'Kill it?' George said to his mates, 'I thought the bloody thing would kill me!' As they were now frantically searching their own bed spaces for snakes, they took no notice of George.

He saw the cook returning, thankfully without the snake, and called him over. 'What did you mean, "No kill snake", asked George, lapsing into the English expression used by the cook. 'Ah, sahib, you kill snake, it mate come looking, kill you!' Since the cook appeared to want to chat, George asked him some questions about Kalyan Camp. 'No good place for first time sahib, many "badmash". Come from Nasik City and rob sahibs.' Changing the subject George, who was on his knees packing his kit away, asked what the food was like. The cook settled down in a squat and, assuming the role of guru, said, 'Sahib, first week in Kalyan, get ants in food, sahib throw food away. Second week sahib get ants in food, sahib eats food and ants. Third week in Kalyan when sahib eats food but ants run away, sahib puts ants back in food, where they bloody belong!'

Three weeks later as George's draft finished breakfast before boarding the train, he recalled what the cook had said. He continued to chew on a piece of delicious granary bread, knowing it was full of ants. He was now a fully acclimatized soldier of the British Army in India.

Frank Booton
PROVOST COY 20TH INDIAN DIVISION

We were en route to Singapore when news was received that it had fallen to the Japs so we diverted to Bombay. In no time at all I was sent to Ceylon where I volunteered to transfer out of the Devonshires into the military police of the 20th Indian Division, then being formed.

I did some hair-raising work on a motley collection of vehicles that the Australians had brought out of the war zone with the result that when I arrived in Hambantota I felt I could drive anything. Colombo was a modern town with plenty of attractions, and included a red-light district. The VD rate was of concern to us as we were expected to keep the troops out of brothels.

After training I joined the 20th Division at Ke Baw, Burma. Our formation sign was an Indian dagger on a black background. We had three British battalions, three Gurkha and three Indian. Because we were too extended we had to withdraw towards Imphal, and fought a rearguard action. Then the news broke that the enemy were behind us and attacking Kohima. This was the busiest and most harrowing time I experienced in Burma.

There was one unit that has never had the recognition it most certainly deserved – the American Field Service, consisting of non-combatant US medical volunteers. Many times I saw them drive out under heavy enemy fire to bring back our wounded.

Eventually the time came when we were able to break out of Imphal. Our Divisional HQ was established at the devastated Tamu, and there was only a narrow dirt track cut into the hillside for vehicles with supplies. We manned traffic control posts along this vital route.

It became a standing joke when, as so often happened, one of our motorcyclist red caps would find an agitated sepoy driver standing above a khud and pointing several hundred feet below, saying, 'Gharri nichi, sahib!' ('Truck down, Sir!') And, sure enough, there would be the remains of his vehicle.

On one occasion we lost contact with one of our TCPs and the Assistant Provost Marshal suggested that as a sergeant I should investigate. It was a good 7 miles of twisted tracks to the Shenam Ridge but thankfully there was a golden moonlight and with a little luck, skill and determination I eventually found the TCP where a mass of vehicles was being held up by accurate Japanese mortar fire. Tired as I was I managed to climb up to a basha where there was a field telephone. I made contact with Divisional HQ and, as I could see the flashes of the enemy mortars, did my best to direct our fire on to them. For this I was Mentioned in Despatches.

When I arrived back I discovered they had captured a Japanese. This was a very rare event as most Japs fought to the death. We made a small barbed-wire enclosure for him so that he could not get hold of anything to commit hara-kiri with. We were pretty scruffy, being on active service in the jungle, but he was scrawny with only a filthy singlet and torn trousers.

During this period we had a Deputy Assistant Provost Marshal whom everyone called 'Major B & S'. We were well stocked with tinned bacon and soya-link sausages and his morning greeting was usually, 'Where's the B & S?' Eventually he was evacuated to a base hospital where a huge tapeworm was extracted from his intestine.

We reached Pegu on my twenty-third birthday. Rangoon had just fallen to us. Then I received my 'repat' orders – back to Blighty. I was put in charge of just ten junior NCOs to police the shipload of 600 sex-starved soldiers, plus a few nurses who were confined to certain parts of the troopship. My chaps had to look after their well-being. Once I visited a sentrypost in the dead of night and felt something draped round my foot. I handed a pair of knickers to the matron next morning, but nothing came of it.

CHAPTER TWO

'They Attacked Us at Night'

On 12 May 1942, the monsoon burst upon General Slim and his retreating troops in all its fury. The general's rear guard was just leaving Kalewa while his main force climbed hill after hill, sliding down the other sides thigh-deep in mud, soaked through to the skin and shivering with fever.

There was no respite. They continued hour after miserable hour, ill-fed and near to exhaustion. At night they lay on saturated ground beneath the dripping foliage with neither blanket nor groundsheet to protect them from the cool night air. There was only one consolation in all this misery: the Japanese, close on their heels, also fell victim to the merciless sheets of rain, which stopped them in their relentless pursuit.

Slim's Burma Corps was heading for Imphal, the capital of Manipur State, the boundary between India and Burma, 500 miles from Calcutta, 60 miles from the Burmese border. Imphal is cut off from the rest of the world in a basin – the Imphal Plain, 30 miles long, 20 miles across, lying 2,800 feet above sea level, on the sides of which stand jungle-covered mountains. The Naga Hills rise to 5,000 feet, the Chin Hills rise to 6,000 feet while some peaks reach 9,000 feet. Between them is a low-lying swamp ablaze with flowers of every shape and hue: purple iris, white jasmine, the maroon and gold of African marigolds, festoons of lilac creeper, primulas and asters, lupins and snapdragons. But not far away, seen through gaps in the jungle, Typhus Hill testified to the deceptive beauty of the region.

Imphal, surrounded by magnificent countryside, was a paradise and the last place anyone would choose as a battlefield. And yet it was here in 1944 that the Japanese, British, Indians, East and West Africans and Gurkhas met to inflict mayhem on each other, to kill and be killed in their thousands. The Japanese were driven by the misguided notion that they could invade India; the others by the need to deprive them of their dream.

But that campaign was two years away. Now, on the last day of that incredible 900 mile retreat, General Slim stood beside the road leading to Imphal, India and safety, while the rear guard of his Burma Corps, still recognizable as a fighting force, filed by in weary platoons.

DAWN

Dawn on the Mayu Range
Is always new and beautiful and strange
To you; because the night before
You're never absolutely sure
The day just passed
Was not your last.
And so the early golden ray
That brings you yet another day
Evokes a silent grateful prayer:
It's nice – to find that you're still there.

Sergeant C. Grimes
29 June 1944

D. Cobb
WATER TRANSPORT COY RASC

We went out to Singapore just as war broke out, sailing on the *Empress of Canada*. I believe she was sunk on her return journey.

Life was peaceful at Kuala Lumpur until the Japanese began their drive through Malaya. We immediately transferred all our gear to Singapore – the so-called impregnable island fortress. It was chaotic there but we pitched in to help. I volunteered to join the Water Transport Company and our time was spent loading everything and anything that looked expendable on to fishing boats. While dumping it in the sea we were constantly strafed by Japanese fighters.

Singapore surrendered in February 1942. A British colonel was keen to get away before being captured and managed to find a launch along the coast where the bombing was less intense. Three days after the actual surrender we set off for Sumatra, travelling by night and hiding out during daylight on one of the many small islands.

We reached Sumatra after three days and nights. Sailing up the Gambi River the colonel then commandeered lorries to take us across country. Eventually we found the last British warship to leave Sumatra, HMS *Danae*, and managed to scrape aboard. I shall always be grateful to the crew of that ship – we had been existing on hardtack biscuits for weeks and they gave us a marvellous cooked meal. Our morale improved considerably when our bellies were full! When HMS *Danae* reached Java she was obliged to put us ashore as she had received a signal to escort a convoy to Australia.

Our only hope was an old riverboat collier called *Wuchang*, built at the Tai Koo Shipyard, Hong Kong in 1914 for the Chinese Navigation Co. Ltd. She was about to leave for Colombo, Ceylon (now Sri Lanka). Five days out we were attacked by a Japanese submarine which fired three torpedoes and then crash-dived. The torpedoes ran underneath us as the *Wuchang* was a flat-bottomed craft drawing only 10 feet of water. The Jap sub surfaced a mile astern but made no further attempt to attack us. We thought it was because the sight of our realistic dummy gun mounted on the stern had changed their minds.

Having reached Colombo we were employed building Mountbatten's new SEAC HQ. We harboured thoughts of repatriation as if we were really escaped POWs. But instead, we arrived at Deolali Transit Camp to join the 14th Army. Someone twigged that if we had been captured in Burma the Japanese would have shot us as escaped POWs. So I spent the rest of my time in India with sepoys and Gurkhas.

R. Dunne
16TH PARA BATTALION

The word doolally has always been applied to someone not quite right in the head. Some of my mates contracted this condition soon after we had disembarked from the troopship *Queen of Burmuda* at Bombay. As soon as we boarded the trooptrain it was overrun with pedlars offering for sale really beautiful-looking heavy 'gold' signet rings. We were invited to exchange our own gold rings for these much better articles. Sad to relate, these 'gold' rings soon lost their lustre, leaving our fingers stained black within a few days.

Later we stopped at a station and the train was besieged by the usual char-wallahs, selling everything from biscuits to souvenirs. One chap bought a mug of tea for about two annas, but when the train moved off he was unable to pay the char-wallah. Miles further up the line we halted again and – surprise, surprise – there was the char-wallah holding out his hand for his two annas.

We did a long train journey up to Quetta in the mountains. Transport was loaded on to flatcars, and each driver stayed with his vehicle to avoid any pilfering by Indian dacoits. On the train for several days, attending to calls of nature involved absolute nerve and balance. With your trousers down, it was necessary to balance yourself on buffers and hang on like grim death.

My ideas about hygiene have changed since my days in India. For a tiny sum many of us had an Indian barber, a nappi-wallah, who came to the barrack room at reveille to shave us while we were still in bed. How many he shaved with his primitive cut-throat razor before washing his gear was anyone's guess.

At Quetta we borrowed a jeep and a can of petrol on one occasion and went swanning off into the mountains to visit a hill tribe camp. The females, both

'At Quetta we borrowed a jeep and a can of petrol and went swanning off into the mountains to visit a hill tribe camp.'

'When the Air Landing School was set up at Willingdon Airport, near Delhi, our main equipment consisted of exactly fourteen parachutes and two antiquated Vickers Valencia aeroplanes.'

young and old, ran into their tents, but to our surprise the men welcomed us and allowed some photographs to be taken. This, we were told later, was unusual as many of the Muslims living in remote areas disapproved of photography on religious grounds. Back in Quetta we showed our snaps to a civilian photographer who begged us for copies as they were so rare.

Squadron Leader R.T.D. Smith, AFM
RAF

When the Air Landing School was set up at Willingdon Airport near New Delhi our main equipment consisted of exactly fourteen parachutes and two antiquated Vickers Valencia aeroplanes, built in 1923, and known semi-affectionately as 'pigs'. Cruising speed was about 85 mph with a maximum of about 90 mph. Instead of slowing down to drop parachutists it was always necessary to apply full throttle to get enough speed for the parachutes to open fully. Later we used Hudson aircraft and troops used to exit the fuselage by a slide.

A Christmas card from the Air Landing School, Chaklala near Rawalpindi in the Punjab, where the ALS moved in October 1942.

The dropping zone was a large area of ploughed-up land dotted with scrub. Parachuting then was such a novelty in India that in the afternoons when the drops were being made we always had a crowd of spectators.

Accommodation was so limited that in October 1942 the school moved to Chaklala near Rawalpindi in the Punjab. The RAF did all the instructing. Wellington aircraft were brought in to supplement the Valencias and Hudsons. A year later that dependable workhorse the Dakota joined us. We must have trained many hundreds of Indian, Gurkha and British paratroops, as well as some special agents of other nationalities. The RAF instructors, unlike the soldiers they were training, received no extra pay allowance for their parachuting. They wore just a small badge on the right arm and it was not until the war ended that they were to wear the coveted half-brevet parachute badge.

A tremendous rapport grew up between the instructors and trainees and this high standard of training in the early days established a tradition that has carried over to the two separate training schools of the present Indian and Pakistani armies.

'Oh, we've Bolo'd Pown Milao,
Upar Dekho, Niche Jao,
And we've done our spot of sweatin' on
the square . . .'

SONG OF CHAKLALA

Oh, we've Bolo'd Pown Milao,
Upar Dekho, Niche Jao,
And we've done our spot of sweatin' on the square,
We've trained every bloomin' mob,
And we've cursed the ruddy job,
But we wouldn't swap it if the chance was there.

Oh, we've Bolo'd Zinderbar,
Ki Jai Sat-Siri-Akal,
And Narra-Mara-Hadri plus the rest,
But of all the troops we've had,
Though none of 'em were bad,
Chota Johnny Gurkha was the best.

So keep your Pown Milao,
When you start to Niche Jao,
And always treat your parachute with care,
We've trained every bloomin' mob,
And we've cursed the ruddy job,
But we wouldn't swap it if the chance was there.

'A year later that dependable work-horse the Dakota joined us. We trained many hundreds of Indian, Gurkha and British, as well as special agents.'

Glossary

Bolo'd Pown Milao	Shout 'feet together'
Upar Dekho	Look up
Niche Jao	Going down
Zinderbar	Indian war cry
Ki Jai	Indian war cry
Sat-Siri-Akal	Sikh war cry
Narra-Mara-Hadri	Mohammedan war cry

Richard Spencer
DIV. SIGNALS INDIAN AIRBORNE

I left Britain in January 1942, heading for Singapore. While the forty-two ship convoy was still on the high seas it was announced on the ship's Tannoy that Singapore had surrendered. The convoy altered course for Bombay. From Bombay I was sent to Kedgoan, near Poona. While there I was guard commander of the bungalow where Mahatma Ghandi was under house arrest. I often saw him walking in the garden and chatted with him in the course of my duty.

'While there I was guard commander of the bungalow where Mahatma Gandhi was under house arrest.'

From Kedgoan I was sent with some others to Mhow to train in Morse so that I could be a wireless operator. In the neighbouring state, Central Provinces, a terrific temperature of 134 degrees Fahrenheit in the shade was recorded. They said it was the hottest place on earth.

We used to go to supper in the mess and I always asked for a 'doh egg banjo' (two fried eggs sandwiched between two slices of bread). We kept our drinking water under the bed to keep it cool. It was in a pottery vessel called a chatti. On exercise at Kedgoan we came across orange bushes. The fruit was so juicy you didn't eat it in the normal way but just sucked it till only the rind was left. They were beautiful oranges, unlike anything seen in Britain.

Later we went to Secunderabad. Hyderabad was about 5 miles away and we were told that the Nizam of Hyderabad, reputed to be the richest man in the world, had offered to pay the British troops six pence per day in addition to their regular pay if they would salute when they saw him. But the then Viceroy of India declined the offer. The Raj still held sway.

In Secunderabad I had an Indian servant whom I shared with another sergeant. He was called Francis and we paid him one rupee each per week. For that princely sum he cleaned our boots and brasses, made our beds, put up the mosquito nets at dusk and shaved us, using an open razor. I used to worry that he might be tempted to cut our throats.

Each morning a native came round selling fruit. I always bought one banana, one orange and one mango. Our day began at 5 a.m. and we finished work at 12 noon because of the heat.

One day I received a letter from my mother asking if I could get her some currants. I went to the local bazaar and bought a pound, took them back to my room and put them in my tin trunk, first hiding them in the middle of my set of jungle battledress clothes – two blouses and two pairs of trousers. I locked the trunk and went to bed. Next morning I saw a black line going from my trunk to the door across open ground to a bush about 15 feet away. When I opened the trunk it was swarming with ants. Despite being annoyed I was amazed at their powers of organization. On one side of the long line each ant carried a currant in its mouth; on the other side of the line the ants were returning for a refill. My battledress was riddled with holes. Subsequently I not only had to wear it as it was but I had to pay for it because it was said that I had wilfully damaged HM property!

While I was there I got dysentery. The lavatories were some distance from our living quarters so I just sat outside the toilet all the time. There seemed no point in going back to the barrack room. Eventually I was sent to the Secunderabad Military Hospital. There it was not long before I noticed something black on the wall just above head level. I was too weak to bother about it then but next morning I woke up to find that the black mark had moved a few inches higher.

'I asked the sister, "What are they going to do with it?" She replied, "They'll take it up to the rafters to dissect it."'
Sisters of No. 127 BGH at Secunderabad.

On closer examination I discovered it was a bat being moved by ants. There was a British sister in charge of several Indian nurses. When I asked her what they were going to do with it she replied, 'They'll take it up to the rafters and then dissect it'. I said something about it making a mess over my bed but she said, 'They won't – they don't leave a scrap'. And they didn't.

From Secunderabad I was sent to Dimapur (Manipur). It took thirteen days to get there, eleven on the train and two on a steamship up the Brahmaputra River. It was announced over the ship's radio that strong reinforcements from America were arriving in the area. We soon discovered from the eleven Americans and their one NCO on the same ship that they were the reinforcements!

While at Dimapur I visited a tea plantation and watched the women at work plucking the leaves. Told that I could place an order for tea to be sent home to England, I paid for a parcel to be sent back each month for a year. Later I learned that every parcel except one had been delivered to my home in Hull.

At one point some 12 volt batteries for wireless sets were required at Kohima, which was at Milestone 48. No one thought at the time that any Japanese forces were in the vicinity so I took a 15 cwt American Dodge vehicle to deliver the batteries when no one else volunteered. The road to Milestone 48 wound round the mountains. Suddenly we spotted an arm sticking out of a ditch and got out to investigate. A body was lying in the ditch and I was about to turn it over when I noticed wires running from it to an anti-personnel mine some 3 feet away. It was a close shave.

Having delivered the batteries and obtained a receipt I had a meal with the intention of returning to Dimapur at once. I was about to set off when I was told the Japanese had put up a roadblock. There was no way in or out of Kohima. My visit which should have lasted a few hours lasted a month. I soon discovered that the British troops, about three thousand within the perimeter, were surrounded by approximately fifteen thousand Japanese. The enemy forces were driving inwards to the point where there were Japanese troops at one end of the tennis court of the District Commissioner's bungalow and British troops at the other.

The situation was extremely tense. One night while sheltering in a foxhole I thought I saw a soldier of the Royal West Kent's coming towards me: I waved him over. He dropped down beside me – it was a Japanese. We stared at each other in complete amazement before we began to fight, but in that confined space there was no room to use even a knife. Desperate, I put my hands round his neck and applied as much pressure as I could muster. Eventually he lay quite still; he had stopped breathing. I had never killed anyone before, least of all with my bare hands. It was an experience that continued to haunt me for many years after the war.

For the next five days we had practically no sleep. I was crouched in a dip in the ground with hardly any protection from flying bullets. There were two dead Japanese soldiers quite close to me who had been killed earlier, so I pulled their bodies towards me and used them like sandbags. I had my Sten gun in a firing position facing where I thought some Japanese troops were. One of the Royal West Kent's was running for cover. This time I was careful to make sure that he was not another Japanese. I waved to him and he fell in beside me. I told him to face the rear so that each of us was guarding the other. By now I was completely exhausted, not only from lack of sleep but also from lack of food and water. I must have collapsed over my gun. Then a mortar bomb must have exploded just in front of the two bodies behind which we were sheltering. The explosion brought me to my senses almost at once. I nudged my companion of just a few hours but found to my horror that his jungle green battledress was covered with blood. He had been stabbed in the back – either by knife or bayonet. While I slept the Japanese had overrun our position and must have thought I was already dead, and passed on.

All of Kohima was razed to the ground. The sole reminders left standing of the District Commissioner's bungalow were the chimney stack and a few outbuildings.

The Japanese built a bunker beneath the church and the only way we could get them out was by using a flamethrower. The church was the one complete building left in the midst of the devastation, unharmed except for five or six bullet holes in the notice board. It seemed like an act of God – I thought so anyway.

When the siege was finally broken by the British 2nd Division, after about fourteen days, the relief was tremendous. We had food and water again, dropped by parachute, some of which landed behind the Japanese lines. Ammunition had also been dropped; luckily, those containers which fell behind Japanese lines could not be used by them because their calibre of bullet was different to ours. We were glad to be able to shave again, put on clean clothes and rest.

One of the inhabitants of Kohima who had survived in the jungle came out to meet us. She had a little boy with her. We presumed it was her son. She was immaculately dressed and spoke perfect English. I asked her where she had learned English and she said, 'At the mission school'. At the time, we were trying to make some sort of bed and not making much of a job of it. She got her boy to bring his machete to cut some bamboo to make a communal bed and even showed us how to do it. All the while we could hear grenades going off in the jungle. We thought the Japanese soldiers were committing suicide: it was well known that the Japanese thought it dishonourable to be taken prisoner.

From Kohima we were sent down to Imphal. From there I went with a detachment consisting of myself and a medical sergeant from the Royal Army Medical Corps, in charge of ten men, including two Naiks (Indian army corporals). (Our group should in no way be confused with a recognized Long Distance Penetration group operated by the Chindits.) My job was to radio back any information we might gather. We carried all our supplies on mules and were totally self-sufficient. We went to Tamu travelling through the Kabow valley, which in itself was an unnerving experience as we were well aware that it was all to easy to be ambushed there.

Somewhere near the Fort White area we found ourselves behind enemy lines. The jungle was so thick we had to hack our way through with machetes. We could only advance just half a mile, or at most 1 mile per day. When we reached a Burmese village the inhabitants were not always pleased to see us. They were Chins and liked to be on the winning side. At that time they thought the Japanese were winning, but nevertheless they provided us with food and even posted sentries on the outskirts of the village. If they saw the Japanese approaching they warned us and we left by the back way. Finally we reached the Fort White area and bivouacked there for a few days trying to get radio signals through to Imphal. We made a camp fire at night and slept around it. A pair of bright eyes watched us throughout the night from the edge of the clearing. Next morning we found the footprints of some large animal and decided it must have been a tiger.

While hacking our way through the jungle on one occasion we stopped at a small clearing. I left the group for a few minutes to answer a call of nature; as always, I was carrying my gun at the ready. Suddenly I heard a noise coming from the surrounding bush. I stopped and listened intently and heard the sound again. It was more like a groan. Was it a Japanese? I crept closer and made out the figure of a bearded man lying on the ground among some bushes. There was just a little light from the clearing – usually it is very dark in the jungle, even in broad daylight. I could see the chap was in RAF uniform. He had been injured and one of his legs was black with ants. I hurried back to our group for help and between us we brought him back to the clearing and cleaned him up. We radioed for an airlift and he was subsequently taken to hospital. The RAMC sergeant with us said that the ants had probably saved his life by keeping the wound free of bacteria. What happened to him eventually I never knew, but I would like to meet him again.

We were just south of Kalewa when we came to the fast-flowing Chindwin River. When told that we had to cross it we realized we had no means of doing so. The mules had been left behind by this time and we were carrying our heavy packs and guns on our backs. Although trained for such an emergency, those of us who could not swim, including myself, didn't fancy the prospect. However, there was a choice. We cut bamboo poles and each waded into the river with one pole between our legs. We used the poles to keep us upright and for support, paddling with one hand while with the other we held on tightly to our guns keeping them above the water level. Crossing in this way we drifted about half a mile down river, and once I turned over completely. But I held on firmly to my pole and arrived safely on the other side. Once back on dry land we radioed for instructions and were given a map reference to make our way to a clearing where we could be airlifted back to Imphal. From there we were transported by road to Kohima. Our tour of operations was then considered completed and we were sent back to Secunderabad.

One time I was detailed to take a party of twelve men by train to a destination in India. We stopped at Bezwadi to change trains. There we found a hostile crowd of Indians belonging to Ghandi's Congress Party, who were engaged in passive resistance. When they approached us we unslung our rifles from our shoulders and pointed them to the ground. They stopped in their tracks. There must have been over one hundred of them and they could have overrun us easily. The Anglo-Indian station master, when asked when the next train was due, replied, 'Yesterday's train will arrive in an hour's time.' We waited and the Indians waited. We were relieved when the train eventually arrived and we could clamber on board.

Back at Secunderabad I was offered a commission; this I declined as the only option open to me was to join an Indian Lancer Regiment. What the board did not seem to appreciate was that the life expectancy of a commissioned officer in the jungle was about ten days!

After spending thirty days' leave in the Nilgri Hills I volunteered for the paratroopers and was sent to Rawalpindi. There I discovered men on crutches who said there were more in hospital, all with injuries caused by faulty parachutes. I spoke to a Canadian who had two broken legs, a broken arm and pelvis. He confirmed that the parachutes were unreliable. These parachutes were being made in India where many workers belonged to the Congress Party and so possibly had a motive for sabotaging the parachutes. I asked to be sent back and was severely ticked off for wasting Indian government money and time.

Some time later I was with the 44th Indian Armoured Division and the whole lot was transferred lock, stock and barrel into the 44th Indian Airborne Division. Attached to the Indian Engineers we landed in Burma behind the enemy lines. The gliders were destroyed so the enemy would not know we were there. The engineers blew up bridges and railway lines wherever we came across them while I kept in touch with base by radio. After fourteen days or so a

'Attached to the Indian Engineers we landed in Burma behind enemy lines. The gliders were destroyed so they would not know we were there.'

Dakota landed in a clearing and took us back to base. Having completed our tour of operations we were given leave, and I chose to go to Kashmir.

In Murree I got a bite from what appeared to be a mosquito. We had been told we didn't need mosquito nets being so high up in the hills. Ten days later I was ill with sandfly fever. Dengue fever attacks the nervous system and I was soon back in hospital in Secunderabad. Later news reached me that my father had died suddenly and my brother was now a POW so I was sent home on compassionate leave.

One last memory is of a Sikh havildar (sergeant), who used to call me 'Spencer Singh'. I always got on well with the Sikhs. 'Take me with you,' he said. I replied, 'You've got eight children in Delhi – what about them?' He said, 'Never mind about them. I'll come back with you, I'll look after you for the rest of your days.' I couldn't take him up on his offer, of course, but it was a small reminder to me of the fondness I had for the Sikhs. India is now only a memory.

H. Suttie
4TH GURKHA RIFLES

I started off at Mhow doing a course of infantry signalling then heard that I was to go to Delhi to join a little carrier pigeon section at GHQ – a nice cushy job I thought. But my luck ran out and before I knew where I was I was in the Burma jungle with Wingate's Chindits. We were known as 34 Column, 3rd Battalion, 4th Regiment Gurkha Rifles.

My mate got out of joining the Chindits by pulling a stroke on the medical officer. He had put on a lovely show – bad back, bad legs and bad everything. We were in stitches just listening to his repartee. When it was our turn to see the medical officer he had used up all the excuses we could think of, so into the Chindits we went. It was rough, but looking back we had a sense of humour and comradeship that overcame most of the hardships. To keep our cigarettes dry in the steamy jungle we shared the same pipe and put whatever tobacco we had into it.

SONG OF THE CHINDITS

We are the sword he forged, eager and bright.
Tempered so cunningly, proudly bequeathed,
Tested, unbroken and keen for the fight,
Others must wield it before it is sheathed.

We are the torch he lit, blazing a trail,
Flaming through jungle land, shaming the sun,

Faith shall re-kindle it, no one shall fail,
None shall turn back till the battle is won.

We are the path he made through the unknown,
Straight as a spear at the enemy thrust,
Never again shall we struggle alone,
We are his legacy, we are his trust.

We are the flag he raised, bloody and torn,
We are his dagger that leaps to the kill,
Strong in our hearts is his courage reborn,
He is our leader, the conqueror, still.

Frolik
4 June 1944

Major Stanley Hamilton, MBE
ROYAL INDIAN ARMY SERVICE CORPS

I had been a brigade MT sergeant and was selected to go through officer training, but when I was commissioned into the Highland Light Infantry I discovered I was a very square peg in a very round hole. Soldiering in the Shetlands in mid-winter hardly seemed like fighting a war so I was tempted to volunteer for active service in the tropics. After a long journey round Cape Town, with a month's blissful stop-over in Durban, I found myself in Bombay in July 1942. Destined to be an officer in the Royal Indian Army Service Corps at Kakul, I constantly pestered my COs for over two years to be posted to something more active.

I must have been a thorn in the flesh of HQ because eventually I was sent to 165 Indian Airborne Transport Company at Chaklala as part of 50 Indian Airborne Brigade, stationed near the parachute training school. What an uplifting experience to don the famous red beret for the first time, and another proud moment when I put up my parachutist's 'wings'.

After a spell commanding lorry platoons I was promoted to captain and put in charge of a jeep platoon. We spent most of our time as 'live' crew for Indian Air Force glider pilots under training. It was a hair-raising time for all. Then we moved to Bilaspur, a trip of some 2,000 miles. We had rest stops for the convoy but I remember covering all that distance astride a motorcycle!

At Bilaspur we trained for our role of assaulting the Japanese-held territories. The parachute element was to drop without vehicles and to commandeer these

'What an uplifting experience to don the famous red beret for the first time.' A training exercise for the role of assaulting the Japanese-held territories.

from the enemy. This was to be followed by a fly-in of gliders with jeeps.

It was hard work and we were highly delighted, to say the least, when the atom bombs were dropped and VJ-Day came. I am sure most of us who were in the Indian Airborne Forces still wonder how many would have returned if the Japanese had not surrendered and we had been forced to go in.

Peter Cummins
ROYAL ARTILLERY

My pal Alec and I were of the generation that could see nothing but unemployment and semi-starvation ahead and I bless the day that we enlisted in the Royal Artillery in 1934. The training was hard but we got three square meals a day.

When I arrived in Lucknow before the Second World War, the main part of the unit had gone off for its annual firing camp and so life was – for the moment – cushy. But it took some getting used to having Indian servants to polish our boots and brasses and do all the mucking-out and stable chores. Even more unusual for someone like me, who had only read about servants or seen them on films, was the nappi-wallah who tiptoed into our barracks every morning with his wallet of various things and carrying his little hand urn of hot water, and started lathering and shaving us before we had got out of bed.

Evenings were mostly spent in the canteen run by a local contractor. There were no NAAFIs in India at that time. I remember the contractor's name was Lalter Perchard Charangelal. Funny to remember his name after all these years. But I can't say his tea and beer were as memorable.

We were mechanized when war broke out, so we had to bid our horses farewell. It was all done, I think, in a bit of a panic because instead of selling off some of them they were shot. We were unhappy that they were left out in the open where the vultures made short work of the carcasses.

Together with lots of other NCOs I was now a bombardier. I was posted to Nowshera where drafts of men from England arrived to form 158 Field Regiment, made up of Dunkirk veterans, militiamen and wartime conscripts with a smattering of volunteers. We were on the Assam–Burma border and when the Japanese forces came through and we were driven out, we experienced a hungry and miserable time. But one day our battery clerk Fred Gilbert came up to me and said those magic words, 'Paddy, you are going home'.

Bert Lamb
INDIAN AIRBORNE

Snakes and scorpions I could put up with, also dysentery which put me in hospital, also the dreadful smell from some of the villages and slum areas of the towns. But what used to drive me almost out of my mind were the swarms of gigantic ants that used to climb all over you if you were not too careful. The memory of Indian trains sticks in my mind, too. They were normally of a larger gauge than their British counterparts and the doors always opened inwards and could be fastened back. Probably if the doors had opened outwards there would have been more than the occasional fatality, caused by Indian travellers falling off. Overcrowding on most trains by third-class travellers was normal. Some would sit on the roof with their belongings in a bundle, while others used to stand on the running boards, holding on precariously to the door handles. With inward-opening doors it was quite possible to sit with one's backside in the opening and feet resting on the running board, bracing oneself with a hand on the door-jamb.

Because of the danger of flooding in the monsoon season most of the track was built either on embankments or, if a large area of low-lying ground needed to be spanned, on trestlework or bridges. So there was always something to see except when we travelled over desert. Often jungle appeared in the middle

'Overcrowding on most trains by third-class travellers was normal. Some would sit on the roof with their belongings in a bundle . . .'

distance, mountains in the background, all majestically moving past your eyes slowly while the foreground consisted of mud hut villages, paddy fields, water buffalo, palm trees, huge spreading banyan trees, wayside shrines and the curious inhabitants. It was a whole new world of experience, quite unknown to us, and because it was, we mostly did not interest ourselves in rural India.

H. Eyley
ROYAL ARTILLERY

I was in Burma. There was not a sound to be heard. I decided to take a walk from our battery position and came across a clearing in the jungle that was completely deserted. Draped over the trees were scores of parachutes, beneath which were several gliders, some showing signs of a rough landing. No troops were to be seen anywhere so I suspected a Chindit unit had been flown in and dropped and had disappeared miraculously into the jungle to infiltrate behind Japanese lines.

'Silent, damp, hands clasping knees
We sit, and there is tightness in our
throats.'

AIRBORNE

Silent, damp, hands clasping knees
We sit, and there is tightness in our throats.
The engines thunder and a petrol-scented breeze
Stirs the hair. I have an absurd desire to grin,
But thrust it down, ashamed of levity.
The monster swings its tail, rejoicing in
Its eagerness to fly, raises its voice. It moves
Slowly at first, then in headlong power
Flings itself upwards to the sky it loves.
The slip-shod landscape slides away;
We fear to catch each other's eye, despite
The will to speak. The transport, unaware,
Bears us to battle through the Burma night.

Denis Thomas
23 August 1944

G. Liddell
CHINDIT

I arrived in India in 1940. After staying at the Royal Signals Depot at Mhow in the Central Provinces, I then travelled all the way up to Dera Ismail Kaan in the North West Frontier Province, the perpetual trouble spot of India. With an infantry brigade I went on several expeditions against marauding tribesmen and was later sent to the fortified town of Razmak, where tribal trouble was, if anything, worse.

By now Pearl Harbour had been bombed. The Japanese had captured Hong Kong and Singapore and were virtually in possession of Burma. The Chindits were being trained at Jhansi where I joined them under our brigadier Michael Carver, later known as 'Mad Mike'. After jungle training the brigade moved to Assam where it was split into two separate columns. We flew into Burma in Dakota aircraft and gliders, with the express purpose of blocking the Japanese supply routes to Kohima and Imphal. After completing our mission we then hung around waiting for the United States General Joe 'Vinegar' Stilwell's American and Chinese Force to relieve us. But they never did. So we had to fight our way up to Myitkiyna where Stilwell was. I was wounded on the way up at Maungdo. Fortunately, I was flown out by a light aircraft to Myitkiyna and transferred to a Dakota, eventually reaching hospital in Assam.

Les Thomas
CHINDIT

I volunteered to transfer to the newly formed Reconnaissance Corps and sailed in the spring of 1942 with 45 Recce Regiment to Bombay on the *Dominion Monarch*.

We underwent intensive jungle training in Bangalore then joined 16 Brigade Special Forces (Chindits). The brigade consisted of the Queens, Leicesters, West African troops and Colonel Phil Cochrane's American Force. We marched 360 miles from the railhead at Ledo to Mawlin, north of Mandalay. I spent three months in Burma before being wounded in action at the battle of Indaw Lake during April 1944. The pilot who flew us out in a Mitchell aircraft was none other than Colonel Jackie Coogan, the American film star.

From Imphal we were flown on to Comilla in Assam and I finished my recovery in the British general hospital there before going to the convalescent depot at Bangalore.

I arrived back in Blighty four months after the war ended. It was not a day too soon, as I missed the big upheavals going on at Independence time. But I do

'The pilot who flew us out in a Mitchell aircraft was none other than Colonel Jackie Coogan, the American film star.'

remember passing through a village near Nasik when the Congress supporters threw stones at our trooptrain.

Vic Gregory
ROYAL ARTILLERY

Our regiment, 123 Field Regiment Royal Artillery, did nothing spectacular. In fact we spent most of the time in Hyderabad State on the Deccan Plateau, and were nicknamed the Nizam of Hyderabad's Home Guard! Actually, being reputedly the richest man in the world, he had his own private army. These units served in the war in the Middle East against the Italians and Germans.

We belonged to the 44th Indian Division, part armoured and part motorized and spent six months training for desert warfare in the Middle East, even getting as close to going as that our advance party made embarkation arrangements in Bombay. But then a widespread famine occurred in Bengal, made worse by greedy merchants buying up all the available grain to sell at inflated prices. The profiteers hung on too long and when the grain was finally released they were unable to distribute it quickly enough to avoid thousands of deaths. The government stepped in and requisitioned our transport so all our lorries and drivers went off to Bengal to distribute this vital food.

As part of the 44th Indian Airborne Division we used to lay down artillery barrages just in front of advancing troops performing their battle training. The GOC, General 'Nichi' Down, thought our accuracy was first-class because we caused no casualties!

W. Savage
DEVONSHIRE REGIMENT

We embarked from Liverpool for an unknown destination. We were in convoy with an escort of about thirteen destroyers. After a voyage in sometimes mountainous seas, in which we went way out into the Atlantic (to avoid U-boats I presumed), we eventually reached Gibraltar. This took about eight days and 90 per cent of the troops were quite badly seasick. It was a beautiful evening when we sailed through the straits, with the lights and sailing boats on the North African coast making a lovely picture.

'This was a nightmare ride if ever there was one. It was just a dust track cut into the mountain side – sheer drop on one side, and a sheer rise on the other.'

Twenty-four hours later, at dusk, we were being bombed by German aircraft. We were confined to our mess decks while this was going on, and as our deck was on the water line, it was not a pleasant experience. In the event some ships were sunk, and the convoy scattered.

On reaching Port Said we entrained for Suez in nothing more elaborate than cattle wagons. Six weeks under canvas there and we were ready to embark on the *City of Paris*. A week later we disembarked at Bombay. This was sometime towards the end of 1943. India was a real culture shock, especially when we arrived at Deolali Transit Camp.

Most of our off-duty hours were spent going round the local bazaars. There was much bartering with small stall owners and nothing was purchased at the original asking price. After a few weeks at Deolali we went to Budni, Central India, for a period of jungle training. Where we were going was no longer a mystery! Training completed we were soon off on a rather tortuous journey to Assam, where the Japanese forces were on the point of breaking through into India. The journey took us to Calcutta and then up the Brahmaputra River on a paddle steamer, and then in the back of lorries up to the Manipur Road. This was a nightmare ride if ever there was one. It was just a dust track cut into the mountain side, with a sheer drop on one side and a sheer rise on the other. The drivers were Indian and must have been in training for motor racing. On top of this some of the older hands told us we would be strafed by Japanese Zeros. As there was nowhere much to run to, we all felt a bit apprehensive. But there was no other way – the dust track was the only land communication with the forward troops.

We travelled through Kohima, and arrived at the front to join the 1st Battalion, Devonshire Regiment, 2nd Division, 14th Army. Shortly after we had passed through Kohima there was a fierce battle there in which the enemy effectively cut the only land supply route to the front. Thereafter we were supplied by Dakotas flying into Imphal, and taking out the wounded.

No one quite knew what the tactics were and everything was rather vague. Perhaps it was just as well. We lived in holes dug out of the ground, went on patrols and had a few skirmishes with the enemy. Some little distance from our position there was a hill known as Nippon Hill. It had been bombed and strafed so much there was little vegetation left on it. Orders came to take this hill at any cost.

It was about 4 a.m. on Tuesday 11 April 1944 when we took up our assault positions at the bottom of the hill. Promptly at 9 a.m., three Hurricane fighter-bombers appeared overhead and dropped two bombs each, thereafter continuing to strafe the area with their machine guns. When the Hurricanes left we began our assault. Our platoon had moved round to the rear of the hill where the

'. . . the enemy had effectively cut the only land supply route to the front. Thereafter we were supplied by Dakotas flying into Imphal, and taking out the wounded.'

terrain was very rough. About half-way up the hill we came under heavy mortar fire. Suddenly there was an almighty bang close by. When I collected my senses I realized my leg was broken. But orders had been given that no one should stop to assist wounded personnel so I was left to get back to safety unaided. This I managed to do by sliding down into a gully and up the other side on my behind. Using my rifle as a crutch I finally reached a track where I was met by first-aid men who dressed the wound. Eventually an officer took me by jeep to the nearest first aid post.

That period of waiting for the assault was a tense one for all of us. It was a time for reflection. England seemed so remote and far away. Would we ever see home again? At least I was still alive.

L. Powell
ROYAL ARMY PAY CORPS

In October 1943 we were issued with tropical uniform and topees and sent to Gourock, Scotland, to board the troopship *Orion*. The tropical gear might have been a ruse to hide our true destination from Jerry, but it wasn't.

The Bay of Biscay was terrible but all else went well as we sailed through the Mediterranean – until just off Crete, when we got orders not to undress, have our life-jackets on and greatcoats and packs ready so we could abandon ship if attacked.

In fact Jerry planes flew over the following day just at evening meal time and dropped aerial torpedoes. Two ships were badly damaged and we copped one torpedo just above the water line near B Deck. It was a dreadful experience. But we made it to Port Said, where we boarded a train for Port Suez. From there we marched to Port Tewfik and embarked on the *Empire Woodlark*. Some wag remarked it had been used in making the Charlie Chaplin film *The Gold Rush*.

We were sailing smoothly along in the moonlight and I happened to mention to a crew member that at the rate we were going we would soon reach Bombay. The sailor replied, 'Don't be fooled chum, the steering has gone wrong – we're going back to Suez.' So there we were on Christmas Day back at Suez and with nobody willing to fix the steering. Eventually, some enterprising REME personnel set to and did the job. Almost three weeks later we docked at Bombay. Then we took a two-day journey on a trooptrain to Meerut, where we were welcomed with a severe lecture on how to avoid the brothels!

Ken Flint
ROYAL SIGNALS

The sight of Indian cooks, half-naked and sweating, bending over a mud oven, was the foretaste of what was usually an unpleasant experience for the newly arrived squaddie in India. Food in barracks was usually cooked by Indian cooks, 'bobajis', under army supervision. The kitchens were often outdoors, a line of mud-built ranges close to the troops' dining-room. We queued up with plates to have our meal slapped on to them by the cooks, and then it was a matter of running the gauntlet to the nearest dining table, hunched over one's plate like the Hunchback of Notre Dame, to deter the kite hawks from swooping down to seize the titbits.

Breakfast was often tinned bacon which usually came from the tin interleaved with grease-proof paper. The paper was often as palatable as the rashers. Soya-link sausages came on the menu frequently. They had the texture of high-quality Oxford sausages but they tasted of sawdust in gravy. Eggs were plentiful but they were Indian – the average Indian hen was not much bigger than a large blackbird. There was always a good supply of bread and butter – mukkin, but the butter was usually made from watered-down buffalo milk – not a lot tastier than margarine.

Lunch was known as 'tiffin' and even though the thermometer registered 100 degrees Fahrenheit it would be the British Army's midday meal. Potatoes, cabbage, etc. were the main vegetables. The meat was usually water buffalo and however thinly sliced was always sinewy and tough. The most commonly appearing sweets would be rice pudding enlivened with a dollop of jam and, of course, that great stand-by, jam roly-poly pudding.

The evening meal was known as 'khanna' (an Indian word that has many meanings of which 'food' is one). This was anglicized to 'conner', its contents similar to tiffin.

Rations in the field went by the name of compo, and usually everything was in tins – tinned fruit, hardtack biscuits, tea, sugar and condensed milk. It wasn't bad really, especially if you could scrounge some odds and ends from the locals to supplement the compo.

The British Army 24-hour packs were supplied in waxed cardboard boxes and issued with a folding 'Tommy cooker' which used solid-fuel tablets. With a bit of ingenuity you could make a couple of meals per day to keep body and soul together. But you had to forget making porridge with the oatmeal block. We used to munch it like a biscuit and it was sustaining nevertheless. Generally, all the British 24-hour food had a slightly 'preservative' flavour, which was not improved by the fumes from the solid-fuel cooker.

'But within hail of most barrack blocks would be the char-wallah, with his charcoal-heated burner and a box full of rolls and cakes.'

The US Army dried-food packs, known as 'K' rations, were plentiful because the US sent them over in shiploads for their troops and ours. There was the feeling, no doubt, back in the States, that famines were endemic in 'Mother' India. The taste of preservative in these packs was even stronger than in our own, and the processed cheese was quite unsuited to hot climates. For breakfast there was a solid mixture of ham and egg and one of meats which tasted like an inferior Spam. Sweets (candy) made up quite a large amount of the individual packs and there was always a tiny packet containing four different brands of cigarettes, including Camels, Kentucky and Lucky Strike; the last of these boasted of being 'toasted' tobacco.

For supper the contractor's canteen always did something on the egg and chips theme. But within hail of most barrack blocks would be the good old char-wallah with his charcoal-heated burner and a box full of rolls and cakes. Having been to the cinema or elsewhere it was common practice to go to one's billet and pick up a pialla, and visit the char-wallah. It was one of the few enjoyable times, lounging around in the dark with a mug of tea in one hand and an egg banjo in the other.

Sleeping was always a problem. One would strip down to underpants or go quite naked, with a towel over one's midriff to avoid a chill in the belly. The mosquito net gave some privacy but it was often a matter of tossing and turning for ages until one could drop off. Dogs were constantly howling in the background, not to mention the buzzing of cicada-like insects.

I can recall the night we were turfed out of bed in Karachi when the *Hindustan*'s sailors mutinied. There was a great noise of drumming from the lines where the Rajputana Rifles were quartered. When the word 'mutiny' went round the camp I thought, 'Jeez – those drums! When they stop the native sepoys will attack us. Indian Mutiny Phase II'.

C. Edwards
REME INDIAN AIRBORNE

I recall on the troopship going out the ghastly experience of non-operational plumbing. There was a constant wash of oscillating sewage on the floor of the 'heads' and it required exact timing to step over the coaming (raised frame to keep out water) at the entrance door and make a beeline to climb on to a seat before the tide of sewage swept back. Fortunately, we were young and athletic and usually made it in time!

We disembarked at Colombo, Ceylon (now Sri Lanka), to provide airfield defence around the racecourse which was being used as an airstrip. Food was always uninspiring but I do remember meal times being enlivened later in India, where we had an enthusiastic chap who used to station himself behind a low wall. He used to fling over scraps of food and wait for the kite hawks to appear, dive-bomber fashion, then clout them with a stout stick. Lunch was often bully beef swimming in a sea of melted fat. No wonder many of us had stomach upsets.

I contracted dengue fever and was hospitalized. There was an elevated portion at one end of the ward where a female civilian doctor used to sit most of the day doing her paperwork. The view of her shapely legs beneath her table brought us rapidly back to health, although we were most reluctant to admit we were fit enough to be discharged!

CHAPTER THREE

'I Heard a Twig Snap'

During the Second World War former cruise ships and large Merchant Navy vessels were hastily converted to carry troops. Single and double cabins were used by officers and women passengers, with the holds converted to troop decks by simply installing foldaway bed-bunks, often three to a tier. Troops would struggle on board at, say, Liverpool or Greenock, carrying their Full Service Marching Order (FSMO) and kitbag. For about six weeks, and sometimes longer, they would live out of a large pack. There were no cupboards or shelves, just their packs neatly stacked in a convenient corner to please the eye of the inspecting officer, who made a daily tour of the troop decks.

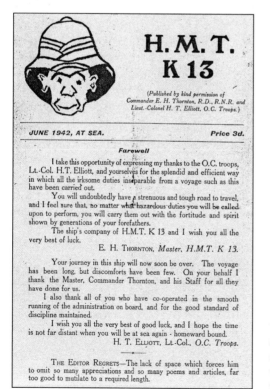

H.M.T. K 13

(Published by kind permission of Commander E. H. Thornton, R.D., R.N.R. and Lieut.-Colonel H. T. Elliott, O.C. Troops.)

JUNE 1942, AT SEA.   Price 3d.

Farewell

I take this opportunity of expressing my thanks to the O.C. troops, Lt.-Col. H.T. Elliott, and yourselves for the splendid and efficient way in which all the irksome duties inseparable from a voyage such as this have been carried out.

You will undoubtedly have a strenuous and tough road to travel, and I feel sure that, no matter what hazardous duties you will be called upon to perform, you will carry them out with the fortitude and spirit shown by generations of your forefathers.

The ship's company of H.M.T. K 13 and I wish you all the very best of luck.   E. H. THORNTON, Master, H.M.T. K 13.

Your journey in this ship will now soon be over. The voyage has been long, but discomforts have been few. On your behalf I thank the Master, Commander Thornton, and his Staff for all they have done for us.

I also thank all of you who have co-operated in the smooth running of the administration on board, and for the good standard of discipline maintained.

I wish you all the very best of good luck, and I hope the time is not far distant when you will be at sea again - homeward bound.

H. T. ELLIOTT, Lt.-Col., O.C. Troops.

THE EDITOR REGRETS—The lack of space which forces him to omit so many appreciations and so many poems and articles, far too good to mutilate to a required length.

'Mess decks had to have two separate sittings, each visited by an orderly officer asking, "Any complaints?"' This troopship leaflet hides the identity of the ship.

For most of the day, unless incapacitated by sea sickness, the men fastened up their bunks and either killed time on deck or else joined the endless, slow-moving queue to obtain a cup of tea, packets of biscuits or a pack of cigarettes at the canteen. The canteen was merely a hatch which a sailor, slowly serving, was often inclined to close at any odd hour without warning. Often the queue, which might stretch along passages and down or up to other decks, was left to disperse when these sudden shutdowns occurred.

Life was a matter of monotonous boredom, made bearable only by falling back on the British soldier's prerogative – the right to swear and grumble. There were few diversions. At night there was usually a film shown and quite often it was a repeat performance as programmes were strictly limited. Of course, the film usually broke down during the performance and there were frequent interruptions by the almost entirely male audience – wolf whistles and shouts of 'Get 'em down!' during the close embraces, and ironic cheers if it was an American wartime action epic. Once the ship entered the hotter climates of the Mediterranean or the Indian Ocean singsongs were arranged on deck most nights.

By then, unfortunately, the food had deteriorated. Mess decks had to have two separate sittings, each visited by an orderly officer asking, 'Any complaints?' But there was no point in complaining, even when the meat was obviously beyond human consumption. Daily doses of mepacrine appeared in tablet form beside each plate at the midday meal. Skin diseases were rife before the ship had reached its destination. Impetigo seemed to be the worst. Purple-stained bodies were increasingly visible where infected parts had been liberally coated with gentian violet.

The heavily laden troopships – some carried nearly two thousand passengers – were in constant danger from menacing U-boats, either German or Japanese. Not all of the troopships reached their destinations. The story of the sinking of SS *Khedive Ishmael* in the Indian Ocean on 12 February 1944 was one of the closely kept secrets of the Second World War. It was one of the worst disasters at sea ever recorded in British maritime history.

The *Khedive*, part of a five-ship convoy, was heading towards Colombo from Mombasa, carrying, among others, eighty-six young women, WRNs and army nurses, some hardly out of their teens. But within a matter of seconds they were swimming in shark-infested waters after a Japanese submarine attack. Only nine of the girls survived. A news blackout of the tragedy was immediately imposed, for a total of 1,297 passengers and crew were lost, mostly East African troops bound for Burma. The tragedy was compounded with frightening results when an escorting destroyer was forced to drop depth charges in among the men and women fighting for their lives in the seething waters. Only 260 were saved.

They had witnessed the enemy submarine being forced to the surface and eventually sunk by the escorting destroyers.

The young women on board had been attending a concert party below deck when the attack began. The *Khedive* went down fast – too fast. Many of the girls who had run to their cabins for a life-jacket found they were trapped. Two WRNs at Trincomalee, Ceylon, heard the distress signals on their wireless equipment. When the extent of the disaster became known both girls were sworn to secrecy. Both knew, however, that it was the convoy which held the next draft of WRNs. Had fate played a more sinister hand, they would have been on that same draft.

A.J. Humphreys
ROYAL WEST AFRICAN FRONTIER FORCE

In 1943 I was lucky enough to get leave to the UK and while I was there my unit moved to India. When a few days out from England I developed another dose of malaria. Malaria usually clears up in about ten days and I had already had the fever part on board ship, so I probably stayed in hospital for about a week.

I had no idea where my unit was stationed and, anyway, everyone discharged from the hospital was sent to Kalyan Transit Camp, about 100 miles inland. BORs travelled second-class on Indian railways and after some time the party I was with arrived at the nearest station to Kalyan. Next morning the new arrivals paraded outside the camp office and in due course the sergeant major marched me in to see the officer in charge. I threw him up a smart salute and stood waiting while he completed some entry on his notepad. He looked up and asked, 'What's your unit, bombardier?' My reply, '2nd West African HAA Regiment, Sir!' produced a deadly silence within the room. The officer, a major, glared at me from behind his desk and then completely lost his temper. 'This is a BRITISH transit camp!' he shouted. 'We don't have COLONIALS here,' and turning to the sergeant major, continued, 'get this bloody man out of this camp at once!' He ignored my plea for help and when we got outside I was told to collect my kit and get down to the railway station. 'Can I have a railway warrant?' 'No!' 'Can I have transport?' 'No! You'll have to walk, we don't cater for your lot!' I thought we were all fighting the same war.

Even though it was only ten in the morning it was already getting hot and sticky as I walked down the long straight road to the railway station about half a mile away carrying all my kit. I was very angry about the treatment I had received and didn't know where to turn for help. At the station, however, I met a real gentleman, the RTO.

He listened courteously to my problem and let me sit in his office while he telephoned to locate my unit. It took some time, but eventually he found the answer: the West African Forces were in a base camp near Poona and my unit was among them.

The nearest station to Kedgoan was Dhond and the RTO gave me a warrant to travel the 150 miles or so. He also gave me ten rupees when he heard I was penniless, or should I say anna-less. This came from his own pocket, he did not have an official fund. Needless to say, I repaid it as soon as I had my first pay day.

After my experience of a 'British' transit camp it was a pleasure to arrive at the West African base camp where I was greeted by old friends. Even the battery sergeant major gave me a friendly smile, but at the same time told me to get to the stores and change that ''Orrible topi for a decent bush hat'.

A pre-war friend was teaching in Delhi and I was given fourteen days' leave to visit him. Delhi was 'out of bounds' to other ranks not on duty, so I travelled in civilian clothes. My second-class ticket enabled me to take one of India's better and faster trains to Bombay. But trains in India need to be seen to be believed. They don't come up to the same standard as the South African train that carried me from Cape Town to Durban, but for India it was one of their best.

Quite often fellow-passengers on Indian trains had something to do with the railway, and my first journey to Delhi was no exception. There were two of them and they kept me informed as we progressed over the 1,200 miles of track. According to their timetable, the trip should have taken about twenty-four hours. But this was India and anything could happen. We'd only been going for an hour or so when the train stopped and the 'experts' told us that there must be something wrong – 'not a regular stopping place'.

We waited and waited and before long everyone was leaning out of doors and windows trying to find the reason for the delay. Some passengers actually jumped down and hurried forward to the engine. The train had collided with one of India's most sacred idols – the cow. It remained in front of the engine until a holy Hindu could perform a purification prayer for the train and, I suppose, all of us travelling on it.

There were no more unusual happenings until we were nearing the famous city of Agra. Crossing the Kunwam River the train again stopped, right in the middle of the bridge. There were three toots on the whistle, meaning someone had pulled the communication cord. Again the information came from a fellow traveller who had the 'knowledge'. We were also told that the train could not stay on the bridge and would have to move before any investigation could be carried out. 'It's in the rule book', we were told.

Sure enough, the train began to steam slowly backwards, clearing the iron girders of the bridge and coming to a halt on the southern side. According to a conversation our railway expert had with the guard as he walked past our compartment, the emergency was caused by someone falling out of the train.

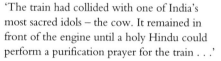

'The train had collided with one of India's most sacred idols – the cow. It remained in front of the engine until a holy Hindu could perform a purification prayer for the train . . .'

The man had been sitting in a doorway and must have dozed off for a second. But it was long enough for him to fall headlong through the door, tumble down the steep embankment and kill himself. In complete contrast to the cow episode, his body was unceremoniously dragged up the bank and dumped on the train. The whole incident took less than five minutes, and we moved off on the last part of our journey.

I'd heard that the Taj Mahal looks best in moonlight, but I can assure you that even in the late afternoon it is one of the most impressive sights I have ever seen. For some unknown reason trains seem to pass the monument slowly and I was able to take a long look at its great marble dome and four minarets.

My fourteen days' leave soon came to an end and I went back to the West African base camp. Our journey from there took us across India to Calcutta; after a whole week in a trooptrain we still hadn't reached our destination. We travelled north-east until the railway came to an end beside the mighty Brahmaputra River. Everyone wondered whether the next step was a swim across the river. Instead, we transferred to an ancient paddle steamer, something like the one featured in the film *Showboat*, with a great paddle turning at the stern. The flat-bottomed boat slowly wound its way north and east until we arrived at Gauhati, in Assam Province, where we transferred to a narrow-gauge railway system. It was not far now, just a few stations to the village of Misamari where our unit had taken over several AA sites from Indian Rajputs.

It must be remembered that in early 1942 the Japanese had poured across Burma and had reached the very frontier of India. The position hadn't changed a great deal between then and the early months of 1944 when my unit took over those gun sites.

Even before the Allies declared war on Japan they had been at war with China. Supplies for Chiang Kai-shek's Chinese Army had been sent via the Burma Road, but now this route had been cut by the enemy it was necessary to carry the supplies by air.

The only way over the Himalayas from Assam to China is called the 'Hump'. Some of the mountain peaks are only a few thousand feet below the maximum ceiling of the American Dakota aircraft used for the job. Our gun sites defended the Yankee airstrips flying these duties. They were also flying deep into Burma with supplies for our own troops, wherever jungle warfare was taking place. Sometimes we were asked to help with these drops, which were mostly free-fall. A dangerous occupation I suppose it was, but our thoughts were always with the lads down below who relied on British and American planes to bring in everything they needed.

Our camp was located on the foothills of the highest mountain range in the world, the Himalayas. There was a very large number of tea plantations in the district and we were not so very far from Darjeeling. Some BORs actually had their leave breaks there. The tea planters were mostly British and very nice people. We, and I include the Americans, were made honorary members of their club and I recall some enjoyable times with them.

'Chalky' White
REME INDIAN AIRBORNE

Not everyone kept a diary of their experiences, but 'Chalky' did, from 13 November 1943 to 1945.

Boarded MV *Highland Princess*, a converted meat carrier from Argentina. Heavy snow. Strange feeling we are going somewhere different as we go up the gangplank. Anchored in the Clyde Estuary whilst the huge convoy assembles. Take a last look at Britain and the snow-covered mountains.

Heading into the Atlantic on a weaving course to avoid U-boats. Sea rough and many seasick but it does not affect me. Find it strange sleeping in a hammock. Food not too good. Boring routine, broken on 18 November when escort vessels dropped depth charges.

24 November   Pass through Straits of Gibraltar. Reassuring to see land again. Next day still in sight of land. Are we going to put in at Algiers? No – but three other troopships did. This evening heavy attack by German bombers. All our ack-ack opens up. Smoke and noise is terrific. Junker 88s shot down by our ship's Oerlikon guns. Yankee troopship left ablaze as shore-based Spitfires chase enemy off.

28 November   Mediterranean Sea calm as a mill pond. Ship's heating system has failed so no hot meals. Living on cold bully beef and fed up with it.

29 November   Three air raid alarms today. Large formations of high-flying bombers. Again a terrific ack-ack barrage put up. *Orion* disappears in a huge mountain of spray and smoke but emerges safely. We join in barrage shooting at the low-flying enemy aircraft with our service rifles. Three planes were brought down.

2 December   Reached Port Said. Weather very hot and smell of the port indescribable. Our unit's kit taken ashore by advance party. We stay on board. Port Said, we were told, is a dangerous place as locals are ready to attack troops found on their own.

4 December   At crack of dawn we go ashore to board a train for Suez. I travel in some discomfort in guard's van. Nothing but heat and sand. On guard duty that night at transit camp with a loaded rifle and bayonet fixed. Two natives killed last night attempting to steal rifles and ammunition.

6 December   Filthy hole and stinks like hell. Troops have to leave Suez by 4 p.m. and look out for knife in back even in daylight.

7 December   Flat broke but officers arrange advance of pay so we go to Suez again with ten shillings each [50p]. Later had a dinner at a place called the Pig and Whistle in Port Tewfic.

11 December   Three days of boredom and guard duty then have to report sick. Find myself in hospital with kidney infection. A smallpox case admitted so have to wait until 22 December for MO to let me go. Special Discharge document states 'recommended for cooler climate'!

24 December Sent by truck to Tewfic to board the *Empire Woodlark* and we steam down the Red Sea. Some way to spend Christmas Eve. Cooler climate – I suppose they think that's funny!

25 December Steering breaks down and we return to Tewfic. Worst Christmas of my life – food and conditions lousy.

26 December In dock for repairs. We kick up fuss but the Scottish troops simply walk off ship. Sailed next day.

30 December Started being sick and had awful headache. Spent most of the time in 'heads'. Admitted to hospital.

31 December Felt better today – temperature only 100! Hospital full of sick men.

3 January 1944 Put in at Aden. Very, very hot. Still in hospital. Leave Aden next day and out of hospital.

8 January Escort ships drop depth charges. Enemy submarines must be lurking in the area.

11 January Arrive Bombay. Had 72 hours just making myself useful on board. Lovely supper of bacon and eggs.

14 January Left Victoria Terminus, Bombay and travelled in crowded train all night. Bribed train driver with some tinned sardines in exchange for hot water to make tea. Couldn't see this happening at home! Stepped out of carriage and on to track when stopped at sidings. Munching a corned beef sandwich when suddenly it was whipped out of my hand by a kite hawk. That taught me a lesson to keep grub covered at all times. Arrived at Secunderabad, rocky and barren, and taken to 516 Command Workshops to be reunited with the rest of my draft.

15 January From January to March I worked during the day repairing Grant tanks. Spent my leisure hours in Secunderabad visiting the Plaza Cinema, the Soldiers' Home or China Restaurant.

After an interesting week as a young REME craftsman, looking after native labour, I was then sent towards Burma via Kaziput, Ammagonda, Wagna and Nagpur, sleeping on stations and in huts arriving at Gaya some days later hungry, flea-bitten and tired.

At Gaya I at least got a pint of beer but nearly lost my head when I bumped into a Gurkha on guard duty. He almost sliced my head off with his kukri.

Three days later, after cholera injections, we marched miles to entrain for a trip to the Ganges. We arrived on our knees.

On 25 April went down a river on a paddle steamer named the *Mohmand*. Had an excellent meal of egg and chips. Arrived at Champur and slept on board catching the trooptrain to Comilla next morning. We then marched 7 miles from Comilla to our new camp arriving dead-beat, hungry and very thirsty.

Up early the next day to pitch tents for soldiers coming out of Burma. We marched to the airstrip to be flown into Imphal but the flight was cancelled. Our kit was taken off us and we were put on board a Dakota loaded with supplies for a jungle drop. The overloaded aircraft struggled off the dusty airstrip. I shall never forget the sight of mountains towering above us as we flew very low over the jungle to locate our dropping zone [DZ]. Other Dakotas were

'I shall never forget the sight of mountains towering above us as we flew very low over the jungle to locate our dropping zone.'

passing us on their way back to base, having dropped their supplies to the Chindits. We pushed the packages out at very low level. Not a very safe procedure for inexperienced troops. Then on to Imphal.

Life then became a succession of one busy and dangerous day following another. I remember getting a long-overdue haircut, receiving letters from home at long last. Then joining 82 Light AA Regiment, RA. The old hands showed me how to make a comfortable bed out of a groundsheet and bamboo.

In May, at Imphal, we had a series of protective boxes. Ours was called 'Catfish Box'. On guard duty at night, air raid alarms, frogs croaking in the jungle, flying foxes in the trees, the sudden clang of a petrol drum cooling off in the night air, gave me the jitters. The enemy made two night raids and set the petrol trucks ablaze. By mid-May we were getting used to it. We built ourselves proper bashas. Even a cinema show in the jungle. But there was still the occasional enemy air raid.

24 June   The supply road to Dimapur reopened and we feel better now. Throughout the siege Dakotas and their brave crews have kept us supplied. We owe our lives to these brave men.

3 September   We leave Imphal in convoy. I drive a 'quad' Ford pulling a Bofors gun. The road to Dimapur is incredible. It twists and turns, very narrow, landslides everywhere and trucks going over into the khuds. We pass through the devastated Kohima. After more than three weeks' travelling we are back in India at Barrackpore, near Calcutta.

Christmas 1944   We are at Ranchi to rest and recuperate. What a contrast with last Christmas. This year the officers brought round coffee and rum before breakfast. There were wonderful meals and plenty of beer.

1945   The first three weeks I am travelling back and forth all over Southern India looking for the unit I have volunteered to join – 14 Air Landing Brigade. I end up in May with 23 LAA Regiment, part of the brigade, and in the last place that God made on earth – Bilaspur, Central Provinces.

Bilaspur camp was literally dug out of virgin jungle. The latrines were just pits with wooden seats and hessian screens for privacy. The pit was burned out daily.

Sometimes we would pour old engine oil and petrol down the pit, then wait for some unsuspecting squaddie to use it. Once he had sat down we would light a twist of paper and drop it into the pit. Scorched backsides resulted from this prank. It might appear heartless but it did help to maintain morale.

C. Buckthorpe
ROYAL ULSTER RIFLES

We had been out on patrol for three days from Haka Camp, Burma. I was carrying the No. 44 radio set on my back. We had changed from voice to Morse because of the range and jungle conditions. Morse carries further over long distances. My mate carried the Morse key and other radio stuff, including spare batteries. In addition to our personal weapons I had an EY rifle, which had a cup discharger attached to the muzzle. Pop a hand grenade into the cup, slip a special cartridge in the breech and the grenade would go further than if it was hand thrown.

On our fourth day out we approached a bamboo swinging bridge over a wide chaung. A message came through that at first light we were to lob a few grenades at the bridge. So we dug a small slit trench beneath the shelter of a hillock. What we didn't know was that an enemy patrol was already covering the bridge. We were ordered to lob over a few grenades and then 'get the hell out of it'. I emptied two magazines from my mate's Bren gun, firing towards the

'On our fourth day out we approached a bamboo bridge swinging over a wide chaung . . . what we didn't know was that an enemy patrol was already covering the bridge.'

general position of the Japanese patrol. They replied with accurate mortar fire, rifles and flares.

We then loaded up Dolly, our mule, with the radio and Bren gun and headed for cover in the dense jungle. Somehow we became separated from the rest of our group and we found ourselves in a dried up river bed ringed with scrub. While my mate Blake tried to make radio contact with the main party, I sat down with my Thompson sub-machine gun at the ready.

Silence prevailed until I heard a twig snap in the scrub. My thumb automatically went to the safety-catch on the Thompson. We got the shock of our lives when the striped head of a large tiger suddenly appeared out of the brush. Not surprisingly, I lost bowel control. I cocked the sub-machine gun in one swift movement, while the tiger stared at Dolly, who was displaying her ugly teeth and braying loudly.

The tiger's face disappeared just as the radio blurted out a message to return. Skirting the brush where the tiger had appeared, and sweating more than the heat warranted, we managed to rejoin our group. No one believed our story. Back at camp near Manipur, I spent some time in the shallow river bed desperately trying to remove the evidence from my body and trousers. While my sprained ankle was being attended to, the MO suggested I had eaten too many green bananas or else had drunk rot-gut whisky called 'Zu'.

Resting my ankle and excused from normal duties, Dolly was hitched up outside. A scratchy record was revolving round a gramophone. It was Bing Crosby singing 'I Haven't Got Time to Be a Millionaire'. Dolly was kicking up her hind legs and braying as if she enjoyed the music. I hobbled outside to see her dancing around the carcass of a 20 foot python. The dead snake was then dragged away to the shoemaker in the nearby village, no doubt to provide elegant snake-skin shoes for several memsahibs.

A vacancy came up on the notice board for a blacksmith. I volunteered and was sent to India on a course. It took two weeks' trekking to reach the Dimapur railhead, then over the Brahmaputra River to Calcutta and thence another long train journey to Lucknow. Lucknow was sheer luxury. Proper char-boys, clean sheets and blankets, soft pillows, pyjamas and – best of all – hot and cold showers.

The work was cushy, just pottering about forging various things on the anvil. This was child's play in comparison to the work I had done at Rustons Forge before joining up. We had a typical Anglo-Indian supervisor in a white suit and solar topee, who came round at intervals to blow a whistle for conna time. The two Indian sepoys with me chewed betel nuts all the time, made their own chapattis and char on site, and quite often would disappear into town to meet their bibis. But I was having a good time. No more yellow mepacrine tablets to take every day against malaria. Gradually my complexion returned from bright yellow to a pinky-brown. There were plenty of vegetables and fresh meat, also fish and chips in the canteen plus the ever popular egg banjo.

Six months' backpay and Japanese Campaign Allowance, combined with a rest from front line action – I was in heaven. Obviously, sooner or later the war would catch up with me, but meanwhile it was a case of living for the present and enjoying the respite of relaxation in the bosom of Mother India.

Alan Turner
PATHFINDER COMPANY

Christmas 1944, Kota Camp, Bilaspur. Some of us decided we preferred fresh beef on the menu so A Platoon nominated a team of ten men to catch a bullock. With three ropes between us we thought it would be easy to lasso the beast. Half an hour spent chasing it and we were completely exhausted. Men from the rest of the company joined in the chase and eventually we got it lassoed, for by now the bullock was exhausted too and was ready to lie down.

There was a small brick building near the guard tent and conveniently fixed to the ceiling was a strong pulley. The unfortunate animal was manhandled into the building and unceremoniously strung up with a stout rope so that its head hung down. Somehow we managed to find a chap who was a skilled butcher in civvy street. Cutting its throat was not for the squeamish; the noise the animal made attracted Indians from all directions who tried to find out what was going on. Eventually, the CSM called out the guard to help stop the Indians from their investigations. Later on the 'dandi-wallahs' (civil police) arrived to make their own investigation into the commotion.

After all that the beef was nothing to write home about, and although it was quite tough to chew we did enjoy it. But the company commander ordered each man to contribute one rupee to compensate the irate owner of the bullock. As further punishment we were rationed to only two cans of beer over Christmas!

Peter Mortakis
CHINDIT

We were pressing deeper into the Naga Hills, a mountainous region of Assam and the centre of the Japanese drive into India. Our column was a new concept in military operations, the brainchild of General Orde Wingate, and we were beginning to feel the strain of the campaign.

The road, better described as a jungle track, wound through the hills with never-ending monotony. Our packs were getting heavier and we kept easing their straps to stop them biting into our shoulders. The water chaggal hanging from my wrist flapped against my leg. The silence of our march was only broken by the jangling of the mules' harness and the creaking of the leather panniers on their backs. Slowly we descended into a valley although we were still thousands of feet above sea level. As we rounded a bend in the track we could see the head of our column moving along the valley bottom alongside a narrow, fast-flowing river in full spate.

The column was coming to a halt, panniers were being unloaded. My thoughts flew to the blackened dixie tied to my pack. Soon it would be boiling merrily over a fire set between two stones and the hot sweet tea would refresh me and the rest of the platoon, who knew my prowess as the fastest tea brewer in the column.

We lay to one side of the track, our aching bodies cushioned by our back-packs and side-packs. Cigarette smoke drifted up lazily and a low babble of human voices chattering filled the valley. The mules, stripped of their heavy yakdans, stood relaxedly grazing on the greenery of the valley floor enjoying a brief respite from their hard labour. Watching a platoon of Royal Engineers bridging the raging torrent that stood in the way of our line of march, we hoped for a long break before the bridge was completed and we had to move on.

'. . . the faithful old Dak, had dropped supplies and rations. Here also we had eaten some apples that were as sweet as any nectar.'

Behind us was the village of Cheswizumi where just one American Dakota aircraft, the faithful old 'Dak', had dropped supplies and rations. Here also we had eaten some apples that were as sweet as any nectar. What lay ahead now?

The column had started from the railhead at Mariani which controlled the American Forces serving the Ledo Road, and was the supply route to Allied troops in Myitkyina, North Burma and the Mogaung Valley. We had marched right around the flanks of the invading Japanese Army to harass their supply lines from behind.

Our brigadier commanding 23 Infantry Brigade was a man whose appearance fitted him exactly for a role in a Noël Coward West End play. It only needed the addition of a cigarette holder and velvet smoking jacket and the casting director would have seen him as a 'natural'. Instead, he was in charge of operations to create havoc behind enemy lines in some of the most difficult terrain possible – mountainous jungles with some areas quite uncharted and only inhabited by primitive tribes.

The Naga hillmen were a particularly muscular race, scantily clad in short beaded trunks with an apron front. Some of them had on ivory armlets with bright coloured feathers attached and some wore similar ornaments just below the knee. All of them had fascinating jet black hair cut 'pudding-basin' style and with their brown skin and almond-shaped eyes made a striking picture. The women wore shirts with beaded belts and necklaces often made from animal's teeth but were bare breasted – the variety of shape and size was limitless.

There was no doubt, however, we were regarded as friendly because often as we passed through, the Nagas would gather with their womenfolk at the edge of the track to smile and wave to us as we and our mules tramped wearily by in single file.

R. Todd
ROYAL ARTILLERY

We had bivouacked beside a river with a detachment of Gurkha Rifles alongside us. We watched half a dozen of them on a bridge pulling the pins out of hand grenades and dropping them in the water. Downstream the rest of the Gurkhas were pulling out stunned fish by the hundreds. When you are living on basic army rations a meal of fresh fish does wonders for your morale.

'Our Company had suffered there, with wounded and sickness, and we were down to thirty-three men.' A Vultee Vengeance dive-bomber at Feni.

W.H. Davies
1ST BATTALION WILTSHIRE REGIMENT

In the Arakan we had to get down safely off a hill the Japs were covering. I remember a tall Irishman, carrying a Bren gun and extra magazines of ammunition, breaking his braces and belting down the khuds with one hand holding the Bren and the other pulling up his trousers, while the ammunition pouches dangled all around him. He fell headlong down the last few yards while we burst our sides laughing. And yet the Jap could have easily opened fire on him. On one position we dug our slit trenches in double quick time and then sat around for a smoke and a breather. Without warning the enemy sent over a few shells and our corporal got some shrapnel in his shoulder. He blamed me for giving away our position by sitting around in a clean white vest!

We were on a hill opposite the famous point known as 1301. Our company had suffered there, with wounded and sickness, and we were down to thirty-three men. Six Vengeance bombers attacked 1301 on one occasion. I had dug in using a Japanese entrenching shovel (they seemed better than ours), but I told young Thompson to get in the trench while I took cover behind a big tree. The blast from the bombs lifted me several inches off the ground each time.

The company commander often used me for recce patrols or as a scout. Once I was up a tree on observation when he came to explain that over one hundred

Japs had broken through but all except a handful had been killed. We formed a fighting patrol to ambush these few survivors. I sat in my tree and waited. The ambush patrol was covering an opening through which the Japs were expected to show. Half a dozen Japs appeared.

Through my binoculars I saw our chaps getting to their feet and indicating to the enemy that they should surrender. Instead, the Japs took grenades from their pouches, pulled out the pins and just committed hara-kiri.

Later on we went to Razmak on the North West Frontier. I fancy we were the last British troops to be there. The air was so thin up in the mountains it took us a fortnight to get acclimatized. On the days that the main supply road to Bannu was opened we would send pickets on to the hills to give cover along the route. Even so, some cheeky hillmen used to snipe at a convoy. One day an officer had his horse shot from under him, and on another occasion a sepoy co-driver in an ambulance was shot from a range of 1,500 yards! The Pathans were always feuding and killing one another. One of the local tribesmen was given a medal by us for killing his own father who was a thorn in the side of the British. It was little wonder the Russians found they could not control these hill people and had to pull out.

'When the main road to Bannu was opened we would send pickets on to the hills to give cover along the route.' The Razmak to Bannu mail bus carrying Pathan tribesmen.

'The Pathans were always feuding and killing one another.' A Pathan tribesmen gathering at Razmak.

TO A DEAD JAP

No more shall you behold your native land
Nor breathe the perfume of the cherry-flower;
Here you lie dead, whilst your late comrades cower.
Fearing your fate, a hunted stricken band.
No tearful pomp shall make your burial grand;
Perchance the screaming kites will first devour
This mangled form, as in some future hour
Japan will prostrate lie, 'neath alien hand.

The dreams of empire lure the hearts of kings
And so men die – each adds one to the vast
Unmemorial legions of discarded tools
Useful awhile, then worthless, broken things –
Praise claimed you first, extinction at the last.
Knaves call you heroes – History proves you fools.

Captain G.W.G. Driscoll
19 June 1944

Ken Flint
ROYAL SIGNALS

Travelling by trooptrain in India was an experience never to be forgotten. Using
the ordinary civilian trains was usually a lengthy business but by trooptrain it was
a marathon. The scheduled services from the fabulous *Delhi Mail*, the *Punjab
Express*, and so on, to the run-of-the-mill long distance trains, took priority
over the unscheduled trooptrains. In the event, whole units of squaddies would
often find themselves shunted into a siding somewhere for perhaps half a day
while the normal railway traffic continued.

The journey would usually start with troops parading in sections on the
platform. They would then have to load their own personal kit on board and make
themselves as comfortable as possible in the Spartan conditions. There were no
luxury items on board, such as stowaway sleeping bunks, upholstered seats,
windows with ordinary glazing, or even bars to deter the odd dacoit from climbing
into the compartment in the dead of night. They were greeted instead with just a
wooden-slatted form to sit on with the ubiquitous hole-in-the-floor toilet.

After a wait of anything up to two hours or so the train would reluctantly
steam off. Cases of tinned rations and large, yard-square blocks of ice would

'. . . if he fancied a hot meal, it was a simple matter to use the metal binding from a ration box to
fashion a kind of stove to wedge over the toilet hole.' A trooptrain in the Khyber Pass.

have been placed in the carriage before departure, but the latter would soon melt in the heat, leaving the carriage floor swimming with dirty puddles; it was important to place tins of meat in the holes of the ice block, conveniently left by the manufacturer. There was nothing more unappetising than to open a tin of bully beef floating in melted grease.

Squaddies were always warned that in no circumstances should they use the ice for making drinks. The water used in the ice factories might have come from contaminated sources. To ensure cool drinking water was available for the journey we would usually fill our chaggal wherever water was to be had. We would then suspend these outside the carriage by the door handles. Occasionally someone would bring a chatti instead and suspend this by means of a net in the same way. Both receptacles worked extremely well as makeshift ventilation systems on the principle that some of the water would evaporate through the canvas of the chaggal or the earthenware of the chatti. When the evaporative effect of heat and wind was working correctly the cooling was very efficient. Of course, there was always the risk of reaching for one's receptacle after too long an interval, and finding all the water had evaporated.

So it was possible to distinguish a trooptrain from a normal civilian train by the number of chaggals or chattis flying along its length in the slipstream. The chatti, being made of brittle earthenware, might in some circumstances be no more than a few shards after colliding with a passing train. But another indication of a trooptrain might be the give-away trails of smoke emerging at intervals along its length. The British soldier is nothing if not resourceful and if he fancied a hot meal, it was a simple matter to use the metal binding from the ration boxes to fashion a kind of stove to wedge in the toilet hole. Wood from the box would provide fuel and an empty hardtack biscuit tin made a good stewpot. Best of all, the fire would not need to be fanned as there was a natural up-draught from below the carriage.

There was one other interesting way of detecting the origin, if not the destination, of a particular train. If all the troops were wearing jungle green uniforms and bush hats and, more importantly, if they possessed the bright yellow skin caused by regular doses of the malaria suppressant mepacrine, then it was fair to assume they had come from Burma.

Lieutenant Colonel C. Christmas
INDIAN AIRBORNE

I was given the task of setting up an Indian Airborne training school in an old barracks just outside Secunderabad in Deccan. We taught use of small arms, driving and vehicle maintenance, held classes in Urdu and did some pre-

'. . . if all the troops wore jungle green uniforms, and the inevitable bush hats . . . it was fair to assume they had come from Burma.'

parachute physical training. In addition we set up an area for demolition and built an assault course.

To get the necessary instructors I had to visit various Indian and British regiments and always received full cooperation. My own little 'skeleton staff' were Risalldar-Major Sikunder Khan and a similar rank in the British Army, RSM R. Webb, of the Sherwood Foresters, and my trusty driver Kuman Singh Gurangh. We only had a fortnight to establish the school and Reg Webb and Sikunder worked near miracles to help me – sometimes working far into the night.

By pulling a few strings I managed to obtain the use of two light aircraft from the state forces of the Nizam of Hyderabad. At one stage during the war I believe he donated enough money to buy and maintain a whole squadron of Hurricane fighters. Few Indian troops had ever been up in an aircraft and we made arrangements for the senior NCOs at least to have short flights, giving them maps to report what they saw and where. A typical report comes to mind, 'Sahib, I was watching through the window of the aeroplane and looking down saw a sentry smoking on duty. Upon my return I put this sepoy on a charge'. Another report stated, 'I can report very much as the aeroplane was going too slowly'.

I met my wife in Trimulgerry, she was a lieutenant in the QAIMNS at 127 General Hospital. We married in May 1944, and had our honeymoon at Vizagapitam on the eastern coast. It seemed that all the divisional staff were

'I met my wife in Trimulgerry, she was a lieutenant in the QAIMNS at the 127 BGH – we married in 1944 . . .'

Sister Kay Carton's ward at the 127 British General Hospital, at Secunderabad, Christmas 1944.

there to see us off at the station, and we left on a train with air-conditioned coaches lent by the Nizam. His trains always bore the letters HEHNHSR (His Exalted Highness the Nizam of Hyderabad's State Railway). It was a far cry from the laconic BR used in Britain later on.

Eventually I went on to Rawalpindi to do my parachute jumps and then was on my travels again over hundreds of miles to Burma, China and so on, ending up as liaison officer to an American outfit.

Alex Tiller
SOMERSET LIGHT INFANTRY

We gathered round the radio in the guardroom at Ghorpuri Barracks in Poona, to hear that war had broken out. Our immediate thoughts were that we should soon be sent home. Instead we went to Multan in the Punjab. I experienced my first earthquake at Rawalpindi where I had been sent to complete a signals course.

I was soon recalled from the course as the battalion was to proceed to the North West Frontier, a belt of territory between 20 and 200 miles that divides India from Afghanistan, a tangle of mountainous country with deplorable communications. There were a few roads built by the Indian Government but generally travel was on tracks only passable by camels and pack-mules.

The tribesmen were Pathans, a Muslim people speaking Pushtu, but there were also numerous tribes and sub-tribes such as Mohmands, Afridis, Mahsuds, Wazirs and Orakzais. And since there was really no border to speak of, many of these tall, strong and very proud tribesmen lived in Afghan land. They were all united, however, by the common bond of Islam. They were noted for their marksmanship and skill in the use of camouflage.

The Fakir of Ipi was up to his old tricks once again, inciting rebellion against India and forming 'lashkars', which were small raiding parties directed against the innocent citizens of towns in the frontier area.

Our battalion, part of the brigade operating in the Amedzai salient, detrained at Kohat and went on lorries part of the way to the start point. From there it was footslog.

We captured Gummatti and Daryobe, both large villages with thick mud and stone walls and tall watch towers. The RAF had already bombed the area to try and make the places uninhabitable, after dropping leaflets to warn the population of course. But the army had to complete the job. It was the first time many of us had been under fire. We lost some men through accurate sniping in this campaign and our CO had his horse shot from under him.

When the emergency had receded we went back to Multan. It is one of the hottest places in the Punjab but we spent some time at the hill-station called

Dalhousie with its pleasant climate and glorious vistas of the Himalayan snow-capped peaks. Down again to Multan we then undertook a 200 mile route-march with exercises thrown in for good measure. The officers marched with us. We crossed into the Sind Desert and passed through villages lying inches deep in dust, then crossed over the mighty Indus River by pontoon bridge. But each night, at our bivouac area, our bed rolls and a hot meal were ready for us. Returning to Multan we said farewell to our CO, Lieutenant Colonel Harding, who was universally respected by all ranks and who had turned us into a tough battalion.

By January 1941 we were back on the Frontier again. This was at Gardai, a fortified camp on the road between Bannu and Razmak. Travelling between these two towns was by heavily guarded convoy including armoured vehicles. The fortified camps were there to keep the route open.

The camp was tented with each tent having its own stone wall and the whole enclosed in a very stout stone wall with a guard post at each corner. Three infantry battalions manned the stronghold. We arrived at Gardai in tropical uniforms only to find it knee-deep in snow!

Twice a week the road was opened for use. All the high ground on either side had to be occupied to prevent any ambush. The capture of each hill was a minor operation in itself and we were often under rifle fire. We could never use the same route twice for fear the Pathans would be on us like a flash. There was the occasion we formed part of a column to relieve Datta Khel Fort in the Tochi Valley. Normally it was garrisoned by friendly Pathans of the famous Tochi Scouts. We were advancing along the side of a hill when we came under fierce small arms fire from across the valley. Bullets were striking the ground all around us so obviously the tribesman had the range. But our officers urged, 'Keep going – Keep going!' and soon the bullets began to go well over our heads. The tribesman had not realized he was on target and had lifted his sights. We lost fourteen men killed at Gardai Camp. It did not go unnoticed, however, that for service on the North West Frontier, the Devonshire Regiment wore the NWF campaign medal. We thought we would be entitled to it also. But no. The medal was discontinued when war broke out!

Our nine-months' uncomfortable tour of duty over, we were driven to Bannu to catch the narrow-gauge railway to Mari Indus. Then on to Delhi and comparative civilization. Little did we know what was in store for us.

In early 1942 we were in Nagpur, Central Provinces, training in jungle warfare. By now I was a signals platoon sergeant working under Lieutenant Philip Pasterfield, who became Bishop of Crediton after the war.

I remember being spruced up for a special parade when Field Marshal Wavell came to inspect us. He stood on a large box and told everyone to gather round. We would soon be going to Burma and he pointed out, perhaps tongue in cheek, that the Japanese were not the invincible soldiers their early conquests made them seem.

The day came when the battalion entrained for the long journey to Calcutta where the 7th Indian Division, under Major General Messervy was formed. The battalion sailed in a Netherlands ship, the *Melchior Triube* during daylight to avoid the many uncharted sandbars in the Ganges Delta. Thereafter we were fully blacked out because Japanese submarines were lurking in the area. We remained apprehensive throughout until we eventually saw, with some relief, the port of Chittagong in the bright sunlight.

The enemy was still on the offensive in Burma. Lorries took us to the scene of operations and then we marched forward in open order following dust tracks at first. It was not long before we were cutting our way through jungle using 'pangas' which are very sharp knives. Occasional indiscriminate bombing by enemy aircraft broke the silence of the jungle until we reached Mount Victoria in the Arakan. There we could hear distant gunfire and guessed it would soon be our turn.

'My first sight of the renowned Taj Mahal was unimpressive, until I realized I was looking through a dirty train window.'

Our turn came sooner than we had anticipated. They attacked us at night, screaming and shrieking like wild things from another world. Their mortar fire was accurate, but we held them at this 'Admin Box' confrontation. Eventually I was wounded by a mortar bomb explosion.

I was taken to an advanced dressing station soon afterwards. They told me later that I had arrived slung across a mule like a sack of potatoes, with blood coming from my ears, a splitting headache, partially deaf and blind. The staff at the base hospital were superb.

The hospital board downgraded me to B6 and transferred me to an Indian Army ordnance corps at Agra. My first sight of the renowned Taj Mahal was unimpressive, until I realized I was looking through a dirty train window. Seeing it later by moonlight was something else.

But soon I was back in Burma, conveyed by the usual combination of broad- and narrow-gauge railways, paddle steamer and lorry. Thanks to my signals training I became a supervisor of a telephone exchange in a huge ordnance depot carved out of virgin jungle. This particular depot served both the northern and central fronts and had lines connected to SEAC HQ, US General 'Vinegar' Joe Stilwell's HQ in China as well as to all the fighting units. One of the perks was decent American cigarettes, such as Chesterfields and Lucky Strikes; such a change from the terrible issue 'fags' called Victory V which were alleged – and not without reason – to be made from dried camel dung.

Off duty we could visit Dimapur where once I saw the famous comedian Stainless Stephen. The theatre was open to the sky and was blacked out during an air raid. I managed a week's leave in Calcutta where as a bonus I saw Vera Lynn in a show at the Metro Cinema. Then things began to happen. We were given rifles, guards were stepped up and we heard the ominous rumble of artillery getting closer each day.

In April 1944 I could not believe my ears when told I was due for repatriation. The conflict of emotion left me speechless for days. But by the usual tortuous transportation system I eventually arrived at Deolali Camp to await a troopship 'Bound For Old Blighty's Shore', as the song had it. Travelling to Bombay we were appalled by the destruction caused by the explosion of two ammunition ships and two laden oil tankers. The accident must have been the best kept secret of the war in the Far East. Casualties among Indians and our own forces must have been tremendous. Whole sections of the stricken vessels had been blown over half a mile away. The aftermath looked like a scene from hell itself.

We had a peaceful voyage via Aden, Suez and Port Said, where we picked up three destroyers and pushed on through the Mediterranean at a fair rate of knots. While on board we heard the news that the Japanese were attacking Kohima and Imphal.

Our route purposely took us within sight of the lights of towns on the American eastern coast. But there was a more welcoming sight to feast our eyes on. As we entered the Firth of Clyde we just stood in wonderment at the lovely hills clad in pine trees, the red-roofed cottages nestling here and there. Scotland you were the best medicine ever taken. The first sight of home after all those years away was indescribable.

The following extract is taken from a brown, faded and tattered magazine cutting, which had laid undiscovered in a drawer for many years. It was sent in by a Burma Star Association member.

Vera Lynn had wanted to go to Burma to entertain the 14th Army for some time and eventually set out on 23 March 1944 in her ENSA uniform, together with Len Edwards, her accompanist. They travelled to Gibraltar in a flying boat. It was Vera's first-ever flight and she was air-sick most of the time. They stopped off at Cairo, where they went out into the desert to entertain over 3,000 men of the Royal Artillery.

Then it was back into the flying boat for the journey to India. At Bombay they changed to a land-plane and flew on to Calcutta. Vera visited a large hospital there, which took hours to complete, because naturally she wanted to tour every ward and sit on every bed and chat. It was there she began to really understand the importance of the direct contact, being asked constantly, 'How are things at home?' The next day she discovered she had no voice left.

Vera could not sleep in her hotel for the bedbugs, which bit her just about everywhere. The noise of the hotel laundry below her room did not help either. But next day she was signing autographs on record sleeves at a nearby shop, did a show at an ack-ack site and gave a concert at another hospital. Three performances a day – all in different places, was quite common. It was a hectic time; her voice was losing clarity and she began to suffer the discomforts of prickly-heat and stomach upsets.

Her real purpose of course, was to reach Burma and the 'Forgotten Army'. The Japanese were beginning to be pushed back at last. Vera left India sitting up front with the pilot, in an aircraft which dropped mail and newspapers at two points en route. They arrived at Chittagong one step nearer Burma. Vera was to stay at the officers' club, and her first priority was to have a bath in a tin tub. There was no running water and her thoughts went back to the hand-filled bath-in-kitchen at home before the war. In the afternoon she did a hospital visit, and made all the usual rounds, then put on a show in a canteen. Spending all of the next Sunday morning talking to the 'boys', she really was moved to discover how pleased they all were just to see her there.

She was someone from home, and although she did not know them, they certainly knew her. She did what everybody does when friends drop in for a chat – talked over a cup of tea.

Next day, Vera appeared before about 1,000 men at the local YMCA, signed hundreds of autographs, and had never been so hot in her life before. Then back to do a show for 600 officers. Performances at various units followed each other in a bewildering succession. Then she set off along the Arakan Road. The ENSA unit was now formed into a self-contained unit, a driver, an officer and an NCO, with Len Edwards (with a Smith & Wesson revolver on his hip), and Vera in one vehicle, with a small lorry carrying the upright piano, microphones and public address system. Their first show was at a hospital for African troops, then another performance for about 3,000 lads at a rest camp. The journey had taken more than eight hours and Vera did shows along the way, one of them at a front line dressing station. She went to bed completely exhausted. Vera saw elephants and heard jackals, and did a show in the nearest hospital to the front line, with another at Ramu Airport

Vera Lynn (now Dame Vera Lynn), would never forget visiting five hospitals in just two days, as well as giving afternoon and evening shows, nor the dreadful sight of the poor, maimed patients.

for about 5,000 lads. She slept on a stretcher that night with a mosquito net draped over her.

They eventually arrived back at Chittagong for even more concerts. The audiences ranged from just a handful of men in a small jungle clearing, to thousands at larger venues. At one time Vera was forced to borrow a pair of trousers from a sympathetic Major, as her luggage had gone astray.

She did shows in bashas – the bamboo hut. In fact she often slept in one. In the mornings to wash she simply poured a bucket of water over herself and just used to let the water drain away into the mud floor. After a show at Feni, they moved to Comilla, where General Slim's HQ was situated.

But Vera would never forget visiting five hospitals in just two days, as well as giving afternoon and evening shows, nor the dreadful sight of the poor, maimed patients. On one occasion she was suddenly sickened by the smell of gangrene, of the disinfectants and the utter sense of desolation. Life was ebbing away all around her. She was totally overcome by it all. She sat down on the nearest bed feeling weary, ill and futile. She asked for a glass of water. Someone said gently, 'We've no drinking water, but there's some lemonade if you'd like it'.

OUR COURIERS

O blessed few, on whom Dame Fortune smiles,
Granting brief respite from the Eastern scene;
Hearken a moment e'er you span the miles
That, parting us and loved ones, lie between.

Tell them no tales of shallow, tinsel glory;
Of glamour and romance, 'neath scented breeze.
But tell them just the plain, unvarnished story
Of heat and dust and rain; dull boredom and disease.

And tell them of the brave and uncomplaining,
Who bear the heat and burden of the fight;
Who nameless die; and seek for no explaining;
But serve as simple guardians of the right.

Tell them the truth – in this you have no choice!
Then, through your lips, shall hear again our voice
And now – Good luck – God speed you on your way.

J. Foster
10 January 1945

THE BATTLE OF SANGSHAK

'Who is this Mortar Battery?' people might ask,
    so just listen to the story of the Battle of Sangshak.
'Twas on a Tuesday evening, the sun was setting low,
    when the lads within the perimeter first saw their yellow foe.
They came rushing o'er the hillsides, their faces alight with glee,
    not knowing they would face this Mortar Battery.
Then 'Fire' came the order and eight mortars spoke as one,
    and dozens of Tojos yellow men never saw the rising sun.
The bombs fell right amongst them, a terrible sight to see,
    and the Japs who thought they'd take the fort were screaming in agony.

Their first attack was beaten off but, as always, night must fall,
    and closer to the perimeter the wily Jap did crawl.
But they never got past the Gurkha, those gallant little men,
    and in the morn 'ere dawn broke they had fled to the hills again.
Night and day the Japs attacked the gallant Sangshak defenders,
    but time and time again were driven back, leaving their dead as reminders.
By now one mortar had fired its last bomb,
    its crew gone where all brave men belong.
They knew they would not die in vain, they died to keep you free,
    so when you in England read these words spare a thought for this battery.

They evacuated the position about half past ten at night,
    and staggered through the jungle till morning's first light.
They hadn't washed or shaved for days, no food or water had they,
    but they tightened their belts and set their teeth and carried on the British way.
After ten days of marching, hope flared up anew,
    for standing by the trackside was a British tank and crew.
They escorted them to safety and soon forgot their pain,
    now you'll find this mortar battery back at the front again.
They did not know that word 'surrender', that word to them was new,
    but one of the miracles was how the wounded got through.

Now don't read this and forget it, nay – read it and digest;
    don't give those yellow devils even half a minute's rest.
Kill them when you meet them, blast them night and day,
    bomb the yellow hides off them from Tokio to Mandalay,
And when they scream for mercy, think of our lads at Sangshak,
    then collect the pieces, except the PEACE that we'll take back.

Anon.
158 Jungle Field Regiment 1944

CHAPTER FOUR

'A Sort of Indian Rope Trick'

The 14th Army's slow and ponderous action against a tough, vicious and sometimes courageous foe often meant hand-to-hand fighting in appalling conditions. The terrain in which most battles were fought was usually thick, rain-sodden jungle where the high humidity and endemic diseases such as malaria, dysentery and scrub typhus exacerbated the tortuous nature of engagements.

The seriously wounded lay for hours where they fell, unable to move, waiting for a medical team to find them. Some were never found while others bled to death before medical help arrived. As if that were not enough, those who had had the good fortune to be taken to a first aid post were in fear of being overrun by advancing Japanese. When that happened, as it did on numerous occasions, the Japanese soldiers bayonetted them where they lay. Such wicked savagery on the part of the ordinary Japanese soldier was never understood.

The more fortunate were moved to the Forward Area Hospitals, eleven of which worked with the 14th Army. They catered for the regiments moving up through Burma. Their sick and wounded were passed back either by mule, jeep and trucks or sometimes by aircraft. Four of these hospitals were just on the border of the Arakan in the Chittagong hill tract, east of the Bay of Bengal. Others were located northwards throughout Assam, along the India/Burma border, through Imphal to the Manipur Road and Kohima.

The hospitals, both those in India and Burma, were run by the QAIMNS staff ably assisted by the Red Cross VADs. Their living conditions varied enormously, depending on the area. In the more remote areas the staff lived in bashas built of bamboo interlaced with matting, with thatched roofs, and floors of brick, cement or just mud. In some places the patients' wards were built of the same materials. Electric lighting was a luxury, fans sometimes non-existent; more often than not hurricane lamps were the only means of lighting.

Patients ranged from Indian Other Ranks, to West Africans, British Other Ranks and officers. The best patient was the Indian, who was considered child-like when sick and showed more gratitude for all that was done for him than anyone else.

Indian nursing orderlies at the IBGH at Lucknow, 1945. In the remote areas the staff lived in bashas. Patients' wards were built of the same materials.

The girls, who were mostly British, did a magnificent job under very trying circumstances, where the use of any modern medical equipment was often denied them. Many of them, often barely out of their teens, would carry immense responsibilities quite unheard of in military hospitals back in England. They matured remarkably quickly for their years.

The greatest improvement these nurses experienced was the rapid introduction of the drug penicillin, a new treatment which involved giving intramuscular injections every three hours. It saved many lives. On occasions the partly trained VADs found themselves working in casualty theatres with just a surgeon.

Night duty was the severe test, however. Because of the strains they endured the girls never exceeded more than a fortnight at a time. It was not uncommon to see just one VAD looking after 300 patients, located in three or more different wards, totally isolated from each other. Alone with just nursing sepoys, who themselves required supervision (they would curl up under a table and go to sleep when her back was turned), she had to make out her reports in a stifling office and attend to the seriously ill.

Accompanied by an old Indian bearer carrying a hurricane lamp, the VAD nurse would visit each isolated ward through sand and mud or in rain, sometimes up and down hills covered with trees and dense foliage. Frightened out of her wits when she spotted a snake slithering across her path, or caught a pair of green eyes peering out of the shrubbery, she hurried between wards like a modern Florence Nightingale.

Human nature being what it is, the nursing staff were in great demand socially. Not only were they subjected to the immense pressures of work but, when seeking entertainment in their off-duty hours, they had not at first learned the art of refusing invitations. This problem was especially prevalent in the tea plantation areas of Assam where there were clubs, tennis courts, dancing and cinemas. They all too frequently got over-tired as a result. They also experienced difficulties in keeping at arm's length the type of man with whom, for obvious reasons, they did not wish to associate.

The VADs in particular, working beside the QA sisters, matrons and the doctors and surgeons, were enthusiastic in their new role and their morale was excellent. They enjoyed their work (and pay), despite the many hardships. The further forward they were to the battle zone the better they liked it and, in some respects, considered themselves lucky to have been chosen to work in the more active fields of service.

The feeling that they wished to be attached to the 14th Army and move up with it seemed more important than the shops, bazaars, trains and buses, the club-life and dances. With few exceptions, although they were ready to have a good time and make the most of their opportunities, the majority of the QAs and VADs put their hospital work first.

Helen Price
CIVILIAN ATTACHED INDIAN ARMY

The Indian adventure was really beginning. We were docking in Bombay. Old hands had already pointed out the 'Gateway to India', a kind of Roman triumphal arch, at the entrance of the Taj Hotel, a landmark, as the ship entered the harbour.

A group of thirteen physiotherapists, dubbed 'civilian attached', we had been five weeks at sea, on the troopship SS *Alcantara*, from Glasgow, and now here it was, the mysterious East. The trouble was, it didn't look a bit exciting, in fact, it looked exactly like Glasgow dockland which we had left at the beginning of June – it had been raining then, too.

The *Alcantara* had been a luxury cruise ship in service in the Caribbean and the dining-room was splendid. I found myself at a table for six, the sexes balanced, and with the ship's first officer at the head of the table. He played father figure/host to us throughout the trip, and pulled our legs relentlessly. The ship's crew was, of course, Merchant Navy.

For years we had been on strict rationing, and here, before our eyes, were bowls full of sugar from which to help ourselves, and white bread, and as much butter as we liked. The cabins were another thing altogether. A first-class single cabin, with washbasin, had been converted to take nine bunks on three side walls, with just enough room for one person at a time to wash and dress.

Being young, we thought it hilarious. Down the corridor was an ex-baggage room, with fourteen bunks, and no washbasins. The occupants had to queue outside bathrooms and other cabins. On the first morning the keen types were down to breakfast 'on the dot'. The lazy ones made it for the second sitting. It was tough on the early risers, for they were told to come to the same sitting.

And so seven struggled to wash and dress in that cabin, while two snoozed in their bunks for another half hour, and had the cabin space all to themselves.

We needed little in the way of entertainment for it was enthralling to walk round the deck and to identify our fellow passengers. With the exception of a group of female cypher officers bound for the Far East, uniform was compulsory. We also understood that all passengers were under the command of the officer commanding troops. The captain controlled the ship and his crew but with reference at all times to the Officer Commanding.

'And so seven struggled to wash and dress in that cabin, while two snoozed in their bunks for another half hour . . .'

My experience of army discipline was not at all what I had expected. After years of hospital hierarchies and pettiness, it was so refreshingly adult. The rules were clear, and also the penalties. One became familiar with Standing Orders and Daily Orders. Ignorance was no excuse.

On board were about two thousand men and two hundred women. Other than ourselves and the cypher officers the women included members of the naval nursing service, WRNS (all ranks), and WAAFs. We were the only ship in the convoy carrying women – a matter which provoked some ribald signals from the other ships.

After the blue skies and dazzling sunlight of the Mediterranean and the Red Sea, we had ploughed through the Indian Ocean for the previous week, watching little clouds speeding along with us, driven by the trade winds. Now, in Bombay, the monsoon was fully under way.

A figure appeared among the dreary dockland 'furnitures', a smart fellow in khaki shorts, knee-high stockings with black tops, a short-sleeved shirt and a very natty pork pie hat – an Indian policeman. So it wasn't Glasgow after all. One couldn't be sure in those days. Our destination was supposed to be secret. Before embarkation many units knew that they were going to the Far East; after all, they had been issued with tropical kit, and we had sailed west for days before turning east for Gibraltar.

At first the convoy totalled thirty-two ships of various functions. Two aircraft carriers had left us for Malta, and we had threaded through the Suez Canal, no longer with escort vessels. Another elegant gentleman appeared, picking his way carefully between the puddles. He had bare legs above polished black shoes, and seemed to be wearing a kind of draped skirt of fine white material, drawn between his legs and hanging quite neatly on each calf. This was topped by a shining white shirt worn outside, the outfit completed with a smart side-cap. With one hand he held up a corner of his shirt, which we now knew to call a dhoti, in the other he held an umbrella. So it was India!

As the ship eased alongside and finally stopped, it all began to happen. The Tannoy announcements, to which we had become accustomed during the voyage, now doubled and even trebled in frequency until they became non-stop. And so it went on, all that day and the next, as every unit of service personnel, fellow passengers and erstwhile companions were told to muster and disembark.

The ship grew emptier and emptier; we waited for our call but it didn't come. Later that afternoon, the senior naval officer in charge of troops was beginning to be tired of the sight of us. He had dozens of female passengers he just couldn't get rid of, as nobody knew what to do with, or where to send 'physiotherapists, civilian attached, Indian Army'. The WRNS and WAAFs, the army and naval nursing sisters, the WAACs, and the other civilians, 'cypherers' (en route to Lord Louis's HQ at Supreme Command New Delhi), were all accounted for as far as transport and destinations were concerned. We had baffled the system; signals had been speeding to and fro from HQ all day, but no satisfactory answers had come back. So it was another night on board for us, in the empty, echoing ship, which, just two days before, had been thronged with its human cargo of servicemen and women. Stewards had to be retained on duty, losing shore leave, to look after us. It was eerie, and not helped by a visit from a 'thief in the night' groping among sleepers – at least that's what we thought he was doing!

At the interviews in London some months previously the interviewers had been at great pains to assure us, somewhat to our mystification, that when we arrived in India, 'they' would know all about us – so this wasn't the first time there had been this little problem. All was well the next morning. We were sent 'in transit' to the sisters' mess at the No. 5 General Hospital, Poona, until our postings were settled. A sister arrived to escort us.

We soon learned the army ways and jargon, but we were not complaining, for every minute held a new experience or, if you like, 'culture shock'. After identification of baggage and transportation by truck and train we arrived in time for tea in Poona.

The sisters were members of the Queen Alexandra's Imperial Nursing Service, dubbed the QAs. Females like ourselves, with civilian status, in common with Red Cross Welfare Officers and other 'miscellaneous' individuals of our sex, were often housed, when necessary, in the sisters' messes. To conform with the Geneva Convention we came under the umbrella of the Red Cross for our protection. No one told us what this meant, but we assumed that it would condition our treatment should we be taken prisoner. Being young, no further thought was given to the matter.

So there we were, having tea – afternoon tea – in Poona of music hall fame. We had dainty sandwiches and cakes, English style, but no fresh milk, something we were not to see throughout our whole time in India. The sugar bowls were covered with little circles of net, weighted down with beads to keep out the almost invisible sugar ants; while the legs of the tables stood in tobacco tins of water, to discourage other varieties from climbing up to reach the goodies.

We were then shown our rooms, from now on to be known as 'quarters'. They were large, high and shady. The windows had overhanging verandahs. Large ceiling fans circled overhead, and the beds had tent-like draperies of white mosquito nets. But the sight which sent us off into girlish giggles were the bath-tubs. An annexe, leading on to the rear verandah, white-washed, and with a bare concrete floor held a tin tub, hip-bath size, which stood on a kind of shallow trough to trap the waste water. This was channelled through a hole in the wall.

Half-way up the same wall was a cold water tap; sat in the corner was a wooden box-like object with a lid. It was vaguely recognizable as a commode – to be known from now on as a 'thunderbox'.

Our instructions were that if we wished to have a bath we should go to the back door and shout 'Gusul lao', whereupon a mess servant, called the bhisti, would bring a jerry-can full of boiling water to be tipped into the tub. It took a bit of practice to master the art of bathing. Instead of letting one's legs hang over the sides, one positioned the tub in such a way as to be able to prop one's feet up on the wall, and so immerse the torso. It was quite satisfactory and refreshing. And what could be more simple than to tip the waste water on to the floor afterwards and watch it run down the trough and through the hole in the wall!

The bhisti heated the water in a kind of salamander, on a wood fire, which he tended at the back of the quarters until the call came. The Indian caste system decreed that each servant had his own special job to do in the hierarchy. We learned that the dhobi was the laundryman; the darzi the tailor; while the

'. . . to master the art of bathing, one positioned the tub in such a way as to be able to prop one's feet up on the wall . . .'
Helen Price with nursing orderlies at 135 IBGH, October 1944.

khitmagar worked in the kitchen, and the choki-dar was the night-watchman. The lowest of the low was the mettar, who cleaned floors and emptied the latrines. They were usually good chaps, resigned to their fate and, trapped in their lowly status, often denied education.

After breakfast next morning, an Indian gentleman, speaking good English, appeared on our front verandah, announcing that he was the darzi and wished to know if we would like any dresses made. This was fast work indeed. There we were, fresh from coupon-ridden Britain, and limited to 'uniform and sportswear' and little else; just one trunk and hand luggage. We told him we were only in transit and might move the next day. No problem, the dresses would be ready by tomorrow. This was heady stuff indeed. Materials and patterns appeared out of thin air. Until now we had been wearing a modification of the Red Cross officer's uniform, a navy tailored suit, single-breasted, with four pockets, slit back and fitted belt. The Red Cross skirt was straight, but ours had box pleats. We had white shirts and black ties, and snooty cheesecutter hats with Red Cross hat band, black stockings and lace-up black shoes. The overcoat was navy barathea with a scarlet flannel lining. Our tropical kit included a white felt hat, six white drill coats, six navy cotton coats, and six pairs of white stockings. Our enterprising darzi produced prices which were hard to believe. Five shillings (25p) for a dress, ten shillings (50p) for an evening dress. The Indian cotton on offer, roughly woven and hand printed, was delightfully cool and colourful, and cost about two shillings and sixpence a yard. We ordered a couple of dresses each, and sure enough they appeared next day. The darzi had not relied on exact patterns but could copy anything, and preferred to take measurements from an existing garment. At these prices, and throughout our time in India, there was always something new to wear. One retained a regular darzi, even on our tiny salaries.

As there were two separate armies in India, the British and the Indian, so there were the two separate hospital categories: Indian base general hospital for the British troops, and an Indian base hospital for Indian troops. Some months after arriving in Bombay I was given a free hand to develop an occupational therapy unit within the rehab centre of a hospital for Indian troops at Lucknow. In Lucknow, the Red Cross tried to fill the need for diversion by supplying materials for patients; until then long-term convalescent patients had been left to their own devices.

The Indian soldiers seemed to be patient and long-suffering. I don't remember a single fractious individual. Our hospital was on the route of the main railway network across northern India, and the war wounded reached us by hospital trains coming through Calcutta and en route from Burma. There

'In Lucknow, the Red Cross tried to fill the need for diversion by supplying materials for patients, until then long-term convalescent patients had been left to their own devices.'

was constant arrival and departure. The less serious and long-term cases were moved further down the line as they became fit to travel. We were mainly a surgical and rehabilitation base, and also had a specialized facio-maxiliary unit, generally known as the 'Max-Factor lot', with its own surgeons, dentists and nurses. Some of their patients with jaw injuries had been nearly starving on admission.

The hospital, housed in peace-time barrack buildings, had 1,400 beds. Matron and colonel did their rounds by car – we used bicycles. I never had less than half a dozen working under my supervision and such problems of discipline as arose were a result of the caste system and not due to resentment at having a female boss. We had officer status; the soldiers called us the PT Missahibs.

As a major base hospital we had many official visitors. During my time there we were inspected by Lady Edwina Mountbatten, the Viceroy, Lord Wavell, and the hierarchy of Nepal. Lady Edwina, as always, left everyone dazzled in spite of themselves. Initial resentment in some quarters about unnecessary spit and polish and red tape evaporated in the face of her easy charm. The patients at work in the OT department leapt to their feet in respectful adoration when Lord Wavell

'As a major hospital we had many official visitors. During my time there we were inspected by Lady Edwina Mountbatten.'

stopped to speak to them. One Gurkha was so overawed at meeting the Viceroy that we had to tell him to stand down long after Lord Wavell had left.

Our lives were made pleasant and easy, a taste of the life of the Raj at that level. We had no problems of inactivity or boredom. Our social life was full. There was a continuous round of mess dinners to which we were invited, and thereby initiated into some of the hallowed traditions of the Indian Army.

Ron Holland
REME INDIAN AIRBORNE

It was September 1944. Our draft was packed on to a small boat with two kit bags per man, rifle, Field Service Marching Order worn on top of that little cloth bag with what the army called 'the unexpired portion of the daily ration'; in fact a couple of doorstep sandwiches.

In those days the ordinary soldier was not told what was happening, so it came as no surprise to find we were only on the ferryboat taking us out to the troopship *Orion*. We learned later that our destination was the Far East. There were about eight thousand of us crammed on board and we were part of the first troop convoy using the route through the Mediterranean and Suez Canal, rather than going right the way round South Africa.

To confuse any U-boat commanders plotting our route (and in the process confuse most of our troops on board), we sailed east after leaving the Firth of Clyde, headed north, then north-west and then due west. Had the Far East been relocated or were we off to the United States?

Eventually the convoy assembled and we set off for Gibraltar, which took only one week. Then a week sailing through the Mediterranean – blue skies, blue seas and flying fish. There was a moment of excitement when our naval escort vessels dropped some depth charges. No one knew if it was the real thing or just practice.

By now the *Orion* was a sweltering oven. No cold drinks, although there was just one issue of a half-pint bottle of orange fizz, which usually exploded into escaping bubbles. Fresh water was only available for one hour each morning. Imagine 8,000 soldiers trying to fill water bottles in 60 minutes. There was plenty of fresh, cold water in the showers but it was sea water. Although we had tablets of special sea water soap, this hardly raised a lather and in any case it could take the skin off your body.

'. . . sailing through the Mediterranean, blue skies, blue seas and flying fish. There was a moment of excitement when our naval escort vessels dropped depth charges.'

We then dashed across the Arabian Sea with no escort as the danger of enemy submarines was thought to be minimal. I had read all the stories about India – the Bengal Lancers, Gunga Din, the Khyber Pass and so on, but where now was all the glamour – the elephants, the glamorous and brightly uniformed dress of the Indian Army? At Bombay we marched across acres of railway sidings to get our first sight of a battered and dusty trooptrain.

This shabby trooptrain was our home for three days. Dusty wooden-slatted seats were our beds at night. The magic of India was slowly revealed, however: vistas of huge, empty plains, lush jungles and towering mountains. At each stop there was a mad rush to the front of the immensely long train to fill up a five-gallon dixie with super-heated water. The British soldier could endure any discomfort so long as he could have an occasional brew of char to restore his morale.

The longest stop was for three hours at Agra. A few lucky squaddies were able to see the beautiful Taj Mahal but, more importantly, they got to squander a couple of rupees on egg and chips at the station buffet. Another stop at Bareilly

'Another stop at Bareilly gave an opportunity to stretch our legs, walk into town and witness the traditional display of a mongoose attacking a harmless cobra.'

gave us an opportunity to stretch our legs, walk into town and witness the traditional display of a mongoose attacking a harmless cobra.

Our final destination was Shahjahanpur to be taken on strength of a REME workshop. We never saw the workshop as the unit there actually disowned us. Quite unexpectedly, we were suddenly packed off jildi to Special Force (Chindits) HQ at Gwalior. It meant going back 2000 miles in the direction from which we had come.

Gwalior, one of the main princely states, where the ruling maharajah was entitled to a twenty-one gun salute, possessed a palace which had a pure silver train-set laid out on the table of the banqueting hall. This was used to send round to each guest the cigars and port decanters after dinner. Raising silkworms was one of the main industries and some of the lads visited the world-renowned silk market. But I spent most of my time cooling off in the glorious swimming pool.

Then I was off to Jhansi to join the Chindits. I was to spend two months with 14 Brigade Workshops which, with typical army logic, provided support for 23 Brigade (British, Gurkha and Nigerian infantry). The brigade was deployed on the far side of the Beswarder River, reached only by a narrow causeway and completely cut off during the monsoons. However, it was an idyllic spot with excellent views of craggy hills rising above a luxuriant jungle. I had my first Christmas in India there. No turkey, no plum-pudding and no beer, just Indian brandy which had a nasty after-effect.

By now the war was definitely swinging in favour of the Allies, but with Japan still occupying so many eastern countries none of us expected this wartime festive season would be our last. Some of us crossed the causeway to join 23 Brigade to live under canvas, sleeping on wooden charpoys with just a durri in lieu of a mattress. The brigade was being fattened up with guinea fowl, fresh meat, vegetables and fruit as they had endured near-starvation conditions behind enemy lines. But there was one vital snag. No fresh water was available. Brought over daily by water bowser, six of us shared one bowl of water a day. Sometimes, quite improperly, I would wander off with my towel and a bar of soap to lather up and rinse by swimming in the river. Nobody told me the river was infested with crocodiles, and that we should have had an armed escort!

In my spare time I explored the surrounding jungle and discovered a ruined temple with shrines to Hindu Gods. I could not resist taking a few snaps with my trusty box camera.

The need for long-range operations in Japanese-held territory lessened, while an airborne assault to recapture Singapore was probable. With many others I volunteered to join the Indian Airborne Division. But first the Nigerian battalion was to return to their parent division. I was selected to command the

REME support detachment on their 2,000 mile journey by road to Sholigar in Madras, Southern India.

Repairs to vehicles were minimal for over two thirds of the trip, then an ambulance broke a main leaf-spring. This I managed to repair using a wooden block and plenty of rope lashing – a sort of Indian rope trick, as I am quite sure it never graced the pages of any REME instruction manual. However, the Nigerian driver ignored my instructions to go easy. One hundred miles later he broke a front stub axle. It was an almost unheard of occurrence. So there we were at the roadside in the wilds of India with just one enormous African driver, no food and no money.

As luck would have it, British army convoys were travelling by, but they were all going in the opposite direction and without recovery vehicles. We could only beg food and water. Then I remembered there was a motorcycle in the back of the ambulance. Riding off into the unknown I eventually found an Indian Army military police unit where they satisfied my pangs of hunger. They also told me of an RASC petrol dump in a nearby town. For several days I lived in the small town in great comfort while the ambulance was repaired.

Of course, I should have gone straight back to the Chindits. But life was so comfortable in the sergeants' mess. I helped the Nigerian Division to waterproof their vehicles for a projected seaborne landing in Sumatra before being ordered to return the 2,000 miles back to the Chindits.

It was realized almost immediately that I had volunteered for the airborne forces. Collecting my railway warrant it was back to Jhansi, passing through Bangalore, Hyderabad, Nagpur, Jubblepore and Phopal. The RTO at Jhansi gave me a further warrant to Lucknow where I stayed the night. The next morning I set off in a public bus negotiating rough mountain roads. I was jammed in with Indians who seemed to be carrying all their worldly possessions – bundles of household goods, chickens in crude bamboo crates and water in earthenware chattis. It was a very ancient vehicle and just managed to crawl along at a snail's pace. Once, at the summit of a large hill, to save fuel the driver slammed the gear into neutral and coasted down the other side like a bat out of hell. I remember thinking that if I could survive this then parachuting would be a piece of cake.

Once back at my unit I was given yet another rail warrant and sent off to join 23 Para (LAA and Anti-Tank) Regiment, RA, at Secunderabad. This was my first real taste of barrack life in a cantonment. It was also my first experience of sharing a bearer who polished my boots, brassware on my equipment and blancoed my webbing. When on parade the bearers were there too, and they took the blame if we were not impeccably turned out.

The GOC ordered leave before the serious business of readying the division for action. The general impression was that wherever the assault took place casualties must be heavy and some of us thought this would be our last leave – ever!

Ootacamund, a hill station in the Nilgri Hills was the place I plumped for, a mere 500 mile journey which would take me further south than I had hitherto been. 'Ooty', as it was popularly known to previous generations, was reckoned to be a premier hill station with scenery resembling the Surrey hills. It was a memorable journey because it was early May 1945 and the war against Germany was coming to a successful conclusion. We left the main railway line at Bangalore and squeezed into a narrow-gauge Disney-type train looking rather like a child's toy against the monster of an engine on the adjoining platform. At the terminus a large placard proclaimed 'Germany Surrenders, War in Europe Ended'. It was a good way to begin a fortnight's leave.

But the war against Japan – our war – awaited us, and when leave was over we undertook another long road journey to Bilaspur, in Central Provinces. From there on to Rawalpindi way up north for our parachute training. Bilaspur, in particular, was not a healthy place. Impetigo, ringworm and skin complaints of every kind were rampant. Parachute training provided a break from the depressing camp and wearing the para-wings on my jungle green uniform helped morale. But the assault would be partly glider-borne so we made 'live' load flights in Waco gliders. The atom bomb ended the Japanese war in mid-August, just before my twenty-first birthday. To mark both occasions I was issued with two bottles of beer – to be paid for, of course.

With the inevitable disbandment of 23 Regiment I was posted to a Divisional HQ workshop, where a mixture of Indian craftsmen speaking fifteen languages and adhering to as many customs worked together in comparative harmony.

The Indian Airborne was to transfer to Malir in the Sind Desert near Karachi. It was comfortable there as the American troops had used the buildings. But modern facilities could not alter the dreadfully hot climate. Walking out of a comparatively cool building into the blast of hot air was like walking into an oven.

I had signed on for a sixteen-year engagement, so my interest in a scheme abbreviated to SEWLFROM (Special End of War Leave For Regular Officers and Men), meant that my twenty-eight days' leave could be added to the twenty-eight days of LIAP (Leave In Addition to Python), although nobody knew what 'Python' stood for.

I was soon homeward bound, travelling on the Jodhpur State Railway, knocking 300 miles off the journey across the Sind. The misery of dysentery and a diet of sulphanilamide drugs with water only, did nothing for my morale in the awful transit camp crammed to the brim with over eight thousand troops. When the time came for me to board the troopship at Bombay I just had enough strength and interest to make my way up the gangway. My lasting memory is of seeing a real whale, doing what whales are supposed to do, giving a final wave of a massive tail before diving out of sight.

Frank Browne
CHINDIT

I was a pre-war regular soldier and spent some time with the Sudan Defence Force in Abyssinia before going to the Western Desert. Then off to Crete for that gallant but quite hopeless fight. I returned to Egypt for the battalion to be brought up to strength for the fourth time and then it was off to India for jungle training. We learned how to load horses, mules, heavy equipment and vital stores on to gliders.

The day came in March 1944 when we emplaned into Waco gliders. At half minute intervals Dakotas rushed down the runway, each towing two Wacos. The gliders lifted into the air first and it was touch-and-go whether the Dakotas took

'We learned how to load horses, mules, heavy equipment and vital stores on to gliders.' A six-parachute raft with mule and supplies.

off safely before reaching the end of the airstrip. Heavily laden with Chindits and equipment they climbed into a darkening sky. It was, at the time, the biggest and most hazardous air operation ever attempted. Between 5 and 10 March 100 gliders and almost 600 Dakotas had carried nearly 1,000 troops and over 1,000 mules.

But I can tell you nowhere near that number actually arrived at the dropping zone, a clearing hacked out of the dense jungle. Gliders crashed into trees, fell into swamps, and disappeared down ravines. Can you imagine the sheer size of the job trying to recover animals and equipment from splintered gliders?

All our supplies came by air with RAF officers attached to the Chindit column to fix the drops. After an air drop we were laden down with twelve boxes of the American K rations, blankets, machete, rifle, ammunition and grenades. With our water bottle and webbing we had a fair weight to carry.

Theft of food was considered a most serious offence when the column was on the march. Culprits were given strokes from freshly cut bamboo rods and salt was applied. Witnesses were told to forget they had seen this happen. I think some column commanders were quite expecting to be court-martialled for this drastic and quite unofficial punishment. After all, it is not permitted under army regulations.

But I came through it all safely, for which I thank whoever was up there looking after me. The funny thing is that when I was eventually repatriated back to Blighty I became a despatch rider. I had a crash and ended up in Edinburgh Hospital!

Douglas Wright
ROYAL ARTILLERY

The Japs did not have many tanks so our 6-pounder anti-tank guns were not often used except to demolish the bunkers the enemy were so fond of setting up. Mostly we used 3 inch mortars in support of the infantry. My job as an OP wireless operator took me into forward positions with a FOO acting as spotter. It was reckoned that officers and radio men were fair game for Jap snipers, but I was not hit, mainly because I think the infantry knew we were vital to their safety. They looked after us. At Mandalay we were given a mission to close a crossroads used by Japs escaping from Fort Dufferin in the heart of the city. We went forward with the 2nd Battalion Royal Berkshires with a General Lee tank in support. Unfortunately, the tank took a direct hit from enemy artillery at very close range and brewed up, killing the crew.

We found ourselves in a precarious position, being fired upon from three sides. We laid down a heavy mortar stonk but the Japs would not budge an inch.

We pulled out when darkness came. The next day we tried again and this time managed to reoccupy the position. Then the enemy struck back with accurate 150 mm guns. We took cover in a garden surrounded by high corrugated fencing. When a shell screamed over the fence it vibrated like a tuning fork. I got a hard knock on one leg while the FOO got a knock on his shoulder. We gazed at one another believing we had got 'Blighty wounds' – but it was only debris flying around. Not so lucky was one member of the American Field Service who had a leg blown off.

When our tanks finally entered Toungoo a Japanese military policeman was directing traffic, quite oblivious to our rapid advance. He waved on the leading tank thinking it was one belonging to his side. The machine gunner in the tank shot him down before he had realized his mistake.

THE AMERICAN FIELD SERVICE IN INDIA AND BURMA

The American Field Service was conceived during the early part of the First World War and served on every important battle front in France from 1915 until the Armistice. In September 1939, within a few days of the outbreak of war

Time and again a simple note appears in divisional and medical unit war diaries saying, 'Evacuation by jeep ambulance (AFS)'. An AFS jeep ambulance about to cross the Irrawaddy River.

between Britain and Germany, American Field Service ambulances and volunteer drivers were sent overseas and served with British and French forces until the fall of France.

The AFS was a front line ambulance corps sponsored and supported by public-spirited United States citizens. It was the only front line American ambulance service composed entirely of volunteers who were permanently attached to the British Army. In India their ubiquitous jeeps carrying the AFS insignia – an American Navaho Indian at the wheel complete with head band and feather, were often seen but perhaps not everyone fully understood who they were. General Wavell, C.-in-C. Middle East Forces, asked that the AFS be attached to his 8th Army in Egypt and North Africa from November 1941. They evacuated 150,000 casualties.

The AFS extended their activities by volunteering to provide an ambulance company approximately three hundred strong for service in Burma, and in June 1943 their advance party arrived to make arrangements. They were not, however, equipped and provided with British and Indian personnel until October when the first section moved to Manipur Road.

During the Assam–Burma campaign the AFS were seen everywhere. Time and again a simple note appears in divisional and medical unit war diaries – 'Evacuation by jeep ambulance (AFS)'. All those who took part in the Kohima–Imphal battles, in the fighting march of the 17th Division from Tiddim, in the advance of the East Africans and 33 Corps down the Kabaw Valley and so on, can bear witness to the value of their work, which received the highest praise from medical units. One high-ranking medical officer paid tribute to them in the following words: 'The only fault I can find with them is that they wish to go too far forward.'

The men of the AFS were drawn from all walks of life – artists, lawyers, authors, business men, archaeologists, bank clerks, playwrights, engineers and so on, but many were students, young men who had failed to pass the stringent medical set by the United States Army.

In India, their CO was Major, later Lieutenant Colonel, Chauncey B. Ives, a lawyer, who saw service in Finland, Norway, Syria, Egypt, Libya and finally India and Burma. Captain John Pemberton led them in the early days in Assam and had with him Captain J. Patrick, a Hollywood script writer and playwright. Lieutenant Hugh Parker made a name for himself when he led a party of seven AFS personnel who escaped from the Japanese through the jungle carrying their wounded, when the 17th Division was cut off on the Tiddim Road.

In the early days the company consisted of a Base and an Advance Headquarters in Poona and Imphal respectively, and four sections, each with a lieutenant in command. Of these, three sections each had 25 Cheverolet heavy ambulances and one section was equipped with 24 and later 36 jeep ambulances. Off-duty hours were spent sleeping beneath a jeep or transforming their bashas into a club house, where they were often seen, at no great distance from the Japanese outposts, painting murals of well-known New York night clubs.

At any hour of the day or night, over any kind of road, or no road at all, the AFS could be relied upon to provide an ambulance and crew whenever the call came. The loudest and most indignant protests came from two volunteers with a wooden leg apiece, when they were detailed to return to base as being unfit to stand up to the rigours of the next phase of the campaign.

The American Field Service will always be remembered as a gallant, globe-trotting unit, of whom the 14th Army has written,

> It was the constant plea of the unit that it should be used with the forward troops, and this plea was gratified on every possible occasion. The devotion to duty and gallantry of this band of men were an inspiration to all who came into contact with them, and was only equalled by the tenderness and care they displayed towards the sick and wounded placed in their charge.

'At any hour of the day or night, over any kind of road, or no road at all, the American Field Service could be relied upon to provide an ambulance and crew . . .'

Clifford Bissler
AMERICAN FIELD SERVICE ATT. 19TH INDIAN DIVISION

Although Mandalay had been entered on the 9th, it was not announced clear of the enemy until 21 March (1945). The city area had been cleared by the 14th, and on the same day 19th Division troops had occupied Fort Dufferin, dominating the south-west sector of the city and held by a large force of Japanese. Planes dropped bombs on it for several days and finally breached the wall. But the first infantry attempt to cross the moat and scale the breach was driven back by furious enemy fire. And the second attempt on the 19th was unsuccessful because of the tangle of weeds in the moat. On the 20th the fort was taken. Then the enemy were discovered to have fled, except for a few stragglers who were rounded up within the next few days. Captain Gilbert reported, 'Gerald Murphy and Jack Ries completed a great piece of work in evacuating the lepers from the Fort in Mandalay. Strange as it may seem, the Japs permitted the ambulances to pass but opened up on the very next vehicle that passed. The incident was actually mentioned in a BBC broadcast.'

During the last stage of this attack Clifford Bissler and R.L. Yancey were wounded, Bissler so seriously that he lost most of one leg. On 19 March they were working north of the fort for the RAP of the Royal Berkshire Regiment (98 Brigade, 19th Division). That same afternoon, Yancey wrote,

> . . . a call came through that D Company, which at the time was under fire from the enemy, had received many casualties which had to be evacuated. A jeep ambulance was needed at once. Bissler and I, however, had a Chev. The doctor didn't want to send an Indian driver who had the jeep ambulance, because he didn't know the way to D Company. However, we knew the way so volunteered for the assignment. We reached the Berks and loaded the jeep with casualties. I remained there with D Company to make room for one more patient, and Clifford took the load back. While he was returning to the RAP the Japs began to shell us. Two Tommies, a lieutenant, and I jumped into a bunker close by. The Japs had tossed about four shells over our heads when Clifford returned from his first load. The jeep had broken down along the road, and Clifford ran the rest of the way on foot, carrying a stretcher. We yelled for him to climb in with us, but just then a Jap shell exploded almost on top of us. That one killed a soldier, wounded another, and almost tore off Clifford's left leg. We jumped out to help him, the lieutenant and I, but just then we were hit by the second shell. We hit the ground fast – but not fast enough. The officer was knocked unconscious, while I suffered a slight shrapnel wound in the right leg and wrist. Clifford was hit a second time in the chest.

The Japs stopped shelling, and we radioed back for someone to bring our big Chev. down. It was, however, about two hours before it arrived, for the road back to the RAP was cut by the Japs. We loaded the wounded in, and then they gave me three tanks for support as we started back. The tanks frightened the Japs, and we got through okay. My wound was not so serious, so I took two loads from the RAP back to the MDS on the edge of the city. Bissler, who had joked about not forgetting to take his nearly severed leg with him to hospital as he wanted it for a souvenir, lost the leg when gangrene was discovered to have set in. He cheerfully endured a long spell in hospital in India and was eventually repatriated back to the States.

Throughout the operations immediately concerned with the capture and mopping-up of Mandalay, the AFS drivers, particularly the jeep drivers, did extremely well under the circumstances. Lieutenant Gilliam reported, 'Medical, infantry and staff officers have all made their comments on the sensible and dependable work our fellows did under the most adverse conditions. The whole platoon was commended'.

In the middle of March, Albert and Morrill had been formally presented with Japanese swords by the Baluch Battalion in recognition of their work. The members of the Jeep Section and 3 MAS who served with the 19th Indian Division in its drive on Mandalay were made honorary members of the division and entitled, when on duty with it, to wear the divisional flash. This distinction was conferred on them by order of the Divisional Commander, Major-General T.W. Rees, who wrote,

On the conclusion of the Mandalay campaign, may I send you my own personal thanks and those of the whole of the 19th Indian Division for the magnificent work you have put in for us. All of us, of all races and creeds, are more than appreciative of your courage, your patience, and the great care you take of our wounded and sick no matter what the physical difficulties or how heavy the enemy fire.

On an historical note, the American Field Service Corps of ambulance drivers served in that capacity with American and Allied armies in Africa, Europe and the India–Burma campaign, deploying overseas 437 ambulances and 891 men. Of the AFS drivers, 27 were killed and 78 wounded.

Disabled AFS ambulance driver Clifford Bissler was awarded two Purple Heart medals in December 1989, more than forty-four years after he lost his leg. Since the AFS is not officially part of the US Armed Forces, Bissler was not eligible for veterans' benefits or military citations. One might imagine from their

habit of joining in any war that AFS members would wear an impressive
collection of assorted medal ribbons. Some of them were specially decorated in
the field on a number of occasions, and they are all entitled to wear the
campaign service ribbons of the various national forces with whom they served.
Wearing medal ribbons, however, is not done in the AFS, and so the oldest and
most gallant veteran is no more dazzling to the eye than the newest recruit.

J. Bamford
WIRELESS OBSERVER UNIT, 875 RADAR

After a seven-day journey by trooptrain we reached Calcutta where we formed
seven-man groups of three ground observers, three radio operators and one
handyman; the latter did everything from running the generators to battery
charging and cooking.

We then set off for our observation post in the mountain jungles of Lushia.
No roads of course. It was a hard slog along jungle tracks with the sweat pouring
off you. I was corporal in charge, and we had a year of being in absolute
isolation with only the Lushia tribes to keep us company. Learning that about
twenty years before they had practised head-hunting did not help matters!

In 1943 we had finished our particular job and were absorbed into 875 Radar
Unit on the Imphal-Tiddim Road. Here we experienced bombing, shelling and
infantry attacks. It was quite a change really.

I went up in a Dakota one day to help drop supplies to the ground troops. As
I was pushing a sack forward towards the door of the aircraft it suddenly veered.
I would have gone out of the exit had it not been for a couple of Yanks on
either side of me grabbing a leg apiece and a Canadian pulling me back into the
aircraft by my ankles! I had one other nasty moment in Burma when a couple of
squaddies I had been talking to just moments before were hit by a Japanese
mortar bomb landing only yards away. They were both killed.

Len Atkinson
A COY 2ND BATTALION WEST YORKSHIRE REGIMENT

The 7th Division was already in the Arakan when our battalion joined them in
November 1943. We started to push the enemy back towards the Maungdaw–
Buthidaung Road but they began Phase One of their march on India. We were
sent over the Okay Doke Pass [*sic*] in February 1944. Two days later we were
surrounded and the Battle of the Admin Box was begun. On 7 February the
Japs infiltrated the 'Box' and bayonetted our wounded lads as they lay in the
medical dressing station. We were helpless as we could not fire back for fear of

hitting our own men. In the morning A Coy went in with fixed bayonets to rescue those who might have survived. Ordered to stay in the 'Box' the fighting was non-stop. We received our supplies of food and ammunition and water dropped from the air by parachute.

It fell to the 5th Division to make for Tiddim, operating for the first time in conditions that had always been considered impossible during a monsoon. We were constantly drenched to the skin. Battalions took it in turns to leapfrog one another. The rear battalion would take advantage of a sunny spell to dry their clothes, write letters home and get some rest. I began to write a poem.

THE ROAD TO TIDDIM

Along the road, that leads to Tiddim,
We smashed the Japs, we fought him 'aye',
I also saw my comrades die,
No sound or murmur came from them,
They were heroes, those gallant men.
And when death took them they just gave in,
Those lads who died on the road to Tiddim.

These swampy jungles thick with trees,
We fight to smash the Nipponese.
And as we fight we have no fear,
Just thinking of those we love so dear.
Still, yet we are many miles apart,
We know you keep us in your hearts.
Knowing this we wear a grin,
While we trudge on the road to Tiddim.

And all our loved ones over there,
We think of you in all our prayers.
These rifle shots, those bullets whine,
We'll beat the Japanese this time.
And now the war has reached its peak,
We dream of good old civvy street.
So you folks keep up that chin,
While we fight on the road to Tiddim.

No paper's headlines we have seen,
About the lads in jungle green.
The 14th Army's turn will come,
When the war in Europe has been won.
So for the present we'll carry on,
And in our hearts will be a song.
The song that's in our hearts we'll sing,
As we tramp on the road to Tiddim.

And when the lights go on again,
Please don't forget these gallant men,
Who gave their lives, but not in vain,
So the world may live in peace again.
Those self-same lads helped us to win,
And now they rest on the road to Tiddim.

THE UBIQUITOUS 23RD
A 14TH ARMY OBSERVER, 28 JULY 1944

A record probably unequalled in any theatre in this war can be claimed by the 23rd Indian Division. Its commander is Major General O.L. Roberts DSO, who has taken 'The Ubiquitous 23rd' to most of the fighting fronts of Burma, seen its numbers doubled and halved and consistently maintained its fine tradition of destroying enemy communications and liquidating the enemy wherever he could be found. For more than two long years it has lived and fought among the hills and valleys and on the plains round Imphal.

Three times it has helped to cover British and Indian troops on their way out of Burma. First it held the gap in 1942, when our army crossed the Chindwin River on its way to India. The following year it helped Wingate's men on their way into Burma, and later helped them on their way back from the first and successful mission into the heart of Burma. The division played its part in the 17th Indian Division's withdrawal from Tiddim.

But let's go back to May 1942, when the division moved from Calcutta to the Manipur Road, for the Indian Railway rocked under the strain placed upon it, as it was only designed to serve the tea plantations of Assam. The traveller had to change from broad gauge to narrow gauge, and the narrow gauge was only one way then. This journey was normally completed in just over twenty-five hours, but some units took much longer. For example, 158 Field Regiment, with all its transport and guns, actually took seventeen days, and although this might not be a record the conditions beggar description.

'The traveller had to change from broad gauge to narrow gauge, and the narrow gauge was only one way then.'

The concentration of the division was further impeded at MS42 when the cliff face came sliding down leaving a 100 yard long break. Everything had to be manhandled across the huge landslide. The rains washed away bridges; three collapsed between Omphal and Shenam. It took one troop of 158 Field Regiment seven whole days to complete the 40 miles and they had to haul their guns into position on the Shenam Saddle, by winching them every yard of the last 10 miles.

There are no troops in the whole of the Imphal sector who know this part of the country better than the 23rd Division, which at one time or another has operated over vast areas from Kohima to 100 miles down the road to Tiddim, and on the east flank has watched the Chindwin River from Homalin as far south as Mawlaik, a distance of well over 100 miles by river.

The motto of the Royal Regiment of Artillery, 'Ubique' – 'Everywhere', could well apply to these men. The Seaforth Highlanders were the first infantry troops of the division to arrive on this front. In February 1942, they were sent for a short while to Kohima. With the coming of the monsoon in May, units of the division held Shenam Saddle south of Imphal while the Burma Corps and thousands of refugees of mixed nationalities came through. In the winter the division moved down to the Kabaw Valley complete with one of its brigades which had spent the monsoon period watching the road for approaching Japanese from the east. When the rains came the brigade moved from Sittaung Ridge, from Minthami and from Tamu. Nothing was gained by staying when the enemy could be held just as well further back, for they would have a supply problem and not us.

In the winter of 1943 another division arrived on the front and took over the whole of the Chindwin sector; this allowed the 23rd Division to concentrate on divisional training.

The 1st Seaforths helped to slow down the Japanese crossing the Chindwin River. Later, when the enemy had managed to cut the withdrawal route of the 17th Division it was the 23rd who played the Good Samaritan for the third time. They held off several very determined attempts on the part of the enemy to get to the tail of the 17th Division and counted more than four hundred casualties. Then its troops had an opportunity to fight as a formation and to swing over to the offensive. One action typifies the fine spirit of the men. A force of Seaforths, Punjabis and Sikhs marched for over three weeks through difficult country behind Japanese lines. It took them twenty-eight hours to cover 10 miles and on one night they only managed 2 miles in eight hours. Their objective was twofold: to disrupt enemy communications and destroy any Japanese encountered.

They did it with considerable success. Moving on razor-back ridges 6,000 feet up, they frequently came so close to the enemy that they were able to hear them haranguing each other. It was in this action that one of the finest examples of air cooperation with the troops occurred. The enemy could scarcely get back to their firing positions before our troops went in to the assault.

This brief recital of 23rd Division's achievements must remain incomplete, for the division is still playing a vital role in the essentially offensive operations now being conducted by 4th Corps. It was not for nothing that General Savory had chosen the fighting cock as the divisional sign, with the emphasis on the fighting; that was the spirit required of his men by their commander, a man without fear and a soldier who understood discipline and efficiency.

H.E. Rowles
ROYAL ARTILLERY

I took a Bofors gun through Burma. The gun was taken in tow by an American Ford known as a tractor, which had a four-wheel drive and winch gear that proved essential on many occasions. For instance, we encountered many bridges built of teak, most of which were severely damaged by the retreating Japanese. Some were passable, others were extensively damaged, so the only alternative route was down a river bank, mostly gradients of 4 or 5 in 1, and up the other side. Unfortunately for me, being a spare motor mechanic and number one on the gun, it was my painful duty to help those who failed to make it for various reasons; to either go back and forth bringing the gun up solo or alternatively anchor down and winch up. It was no easy task, I can assure you.

Each bridge had a loading sign indicating the extent of the damage. So at times one took chances rather than unhitch the gun and manhandle it in maybe 12 inches or so of mud or dust. On one occasion we took a chance and passed the sign. The sergeant, being a very intelligent bod, jumped down and stamped on the bridge. 'Okay, Bert, come on,' he shouted with absolute confidence. We were lucky on that occasion.

I remember one vehicle breaking down, and the limber gunner, driver mechanic and one other were ordered to stay and try to get mobile with the hope of catching us up 3 miles or so the other side of the bridge. The road was under shell fire the whole time. By the time they got moving it was dark. They almost flew across the bridge, rejoicing in their good luck. Then just as quickly they went down on two wheels with the gun in the air. There was nothing anyone could do but wait for daylight and hope for rescue. Scared out of their wits, they got their heads down for a nap only to be invaded by baboons.

Rivers were crossed by driving on to sections of Bailey bridges, anchored to Ducks, and up the other side. I have since realized that driving the tractor and gun was quite a responsible job. On one occasion, I remember travelling in the hours of darkness up a mountain pass literally on the edge of a precipice. I encountered a stationary vehicle obstructing me, loaded with Bailey bridge sections. In order to pass I had to cut so close that I tore the canopy and felt one of the gun wheels sliding away. Fortunately, I managed to gain sufficient speed to avoid a disaster. Tractor, gun and crew very nearly ended up hundreds of feet down a valley.

Our main job was protecting the forward airstrips, from where the wounded were flown out and supply drops made. I will never forget driving for over forty-eight hours through thick jungle without ever seeing daylight owing to the great height of the trees and thick undergrowth. On more than one occasion it was 140 degrees in the shade. We passed many villages en route set on fire by tracer bullets where the Japanese and Pongies (Burmese priests who were our greatest traitors) had been hiding.

I must mention the military police, for they were not all men of doubtful parentage. They were responsible for laying the divisional signs and, on many occasions, for directing us to comparative safety. Throughout the campaign we were frequently called upon to put up our Bofors guns and assist the infantry, especially when they were being ambushed close by. This often proved fatal to the RA as we were not fully trained in close combat, while the infantry had been taught to take cover behind a blade of grass!

Ron Demmery
353 SQUADRON RAF

I was a founder member of the unit when it was formed at Dum Dum near Calcutta, on 1 June 1942. We were truly an Allied squadron with British, Indian, Canadian, Australian and New Zealand air crew, although the ground crews were British. On 13 July we became operational, flying the Lockheed Hudson on shipping reconnaissance down the Cheduba Straits and over Ramree Island.

We had a detachment at Cattack where the CO used to ride a white horse around the camp. Being a peace-time man he required bags of 'bull' and insisted the sentries should present arms when saluting officers. We took leave at Puri by the sea, and I recall visiting a Hindu temple devoted, it seemed, to the worship of sex. We were constantly pestered by vendors selling 'feelthy pictures'.

We were designated a mobile squadron and set up a camp of bashas at Dhubalia. The Imprest Officer flew to Calcutta to collect our pay which he deposited in a safe overnight in our basha. A thousand rupees went missing and I got a tremendous grilling because I was sleeping in the basha. But it seems the mistake was made at Calcutta. The whole incident was hushed up as it was a court martial offence to carry money by air!

We moved to Palam in August 1943 and in the following month began a scheduled route from Delhi through to Calcutta with mail, flying over forty trips a month and lost four aircraft in a couple of weeks. I had the sad duty of sorting out the personal effects of the dead crew members.

But the greatest tragedy occurred at Dum Dum where we had a Royal Signals detachment helping us with communications. They had occupied radio rooms at either ends of a block. Our RAF sentries used to assemble in one of these rooms before mounting guard. One particular 'erk' put his rifle in the corner of the room to light a cigarette. A signals radio operator picked up the rifle and, without realizing a round was 'up the spout' aimed it in fun at his fellow operator in the adjoining room. He pulled the trigger and killed his pal instantly.

Fred Stone
2ND BATTALION KOYLI

We had been training in the use of assault boats on this quite beautiful lake fringed with white water lilies. During a break we were allowed to swim, after which we climbed back on board for a smoke. There was a shriek when someone found a huge leech bloated with blood, hanging on to a very sensitive part of his anatomy. All of us descended upon him laughingly offering to burn the leech off with our lighted cigarettes. He would have none of this and said he preferred to do this delicate job himself. But, of course, this always leaves a bluish mark where the leech has punctured the skin. We often wondered what his future bride would make of this 'tattoo' mark on his wedding night!

C. Owen
RAMC 47 BGH

Nowadays some veterans wonder whether all that we endured 'out there' was really worth it. I can say – without doubt – that comradeship and a sense of humour got me through the many tragedies and I would not have missed it for all the tea in China.

The ship carrying all our heavy hospital equipment was sunk and so our sailing was delayed. In mid-ocean we heard the Japs had taken Singapore so we diverted to India. It was chaos. The 1942 'Quit India' unrest was at its height with rioting, tramcars being set alight, and barbed wire barricades and machine gun posts set up throughout Calcutta. We took over the Loretto Convent for our medical cases, where seven hundred beds were available, but during the malarial season there were more patients on stretchers on the floor than in the beds. One of my unpleasant duties was carrying the dead to the mortuary.

In 1943 the crops failed and famine resulted. Bodies were lying in the streets everywhere, and I remember the refuse truck with 'Calcutta Corpse Collection' written on the side, picking them up.

By now we were nursing the Chindits recently returned from their hazardous operations behind Japanese lines. It was a harrowing time, for most of them looked like skeletons and of course, they were riddled with disease. Later we moved up to Ranchi where the field hospital was ravaged by a severe cyclone. Before long, however, we sent home our first man on demob, and then lined up to say farewell (among other things) to our unloved CO, giving him salutes that were not all of the regulation kind!

Then we went to Singapore via Rangoon. We took over the Victoria Hospital and discovered that the Japanese had not made use of it. We all heard the rumour about the Gurkha troops. On hearing what the Japs had done to the Gurkha POWs, they swooped through the Japanese lines exacting revenge with their kukris.

There were some gun battles between looters and the army patrols. I felt no shame in getting down on the floor of the bungalow with shots coming through the windows and roof.

Gracie Fields came to entertain the troops. But it was remembered she would have been the 'Darling of the Forces' had she not left England for America during the London Blitz. When our RSM was approached to provide bed linen for Gracie's accommodation he was anything but helpful and referred her to the Yankee authorities!

Gracie Fields

In November 1939 Gracie Fields far from home and comfort, was boosting the morale of the British Expeditionary Force in France. She gave a series of concerts throughout western Europe, and spent Christmas entertaining the RAF at Rheims, troops along the Maginot Line and then the navy, who honoured her by naming a ship Gracie Fields. Despite his American background, Monty Banks, Gracie's husband, was an Italian, and as such faced internment until the end of hostilities. Rather than have him face humiliation, Gracie decided they should go to Canada. Gracie raised thousands of dollars which went towards the British war effort. Thirteen months later she returned to England, and went from factory to coal-mine, army camp to munitions works, singing with a depth of sincerity at all her triumphant performances. She sang her way back into the hearts of the British people when she flew to entertain from North Africa to Singapore, Mombasa to Rangoon. She was unjustly criticised for quitting Britain, but she returned to give show after show. After one shipyard show, other workers threatened to strike unless Gracie sang for them too.

Stuart Eadon
HMS *INDEFATIGABLE.*
An extract from the book *Satishima* gives all insight into the naval side of operations against the Japanese.

My own diary, which was written up after the war from notes made at the time, reads as follows: 'It was Easter Sunday, 1 April 1945, April Fools' Day. As dawn action stations sounded off that fateful morning, I slipped from my top bunk, partly dressed, grabbed my anti-flash gear and tin hat, called "See you later" to my cabin mate Len, and went up to the weather deck. Along now to port side midships and down over the side of the ship on to my gun sponson. The young Scots boy Arral was clambering down on to his gun to my left and Rowson, who had replaced Inman, was already loading his Oerlikon. I switched on while Rowson completed the covering of his body with anti-flash hood and gloves and then took his seat and swung the track from left to right and the barrel up and down to "warm her up". I went back up the small vertical ladder and along to Arral to check that he was ready.

Our Seafires were already patrolling overhead and the fleet altered course, as more aircraft flew off from the carriers. The dawn had come rapidly and the sun seemed in a hurry to reach its zenith. Our aircraft went further away when suddenly, "Red alert, Red alert" screeched over the Tannoy. It was nearly 0700. The Japs peeled off out of the direction of the sun as our Seafires got amongst them, so we couldn't open fire for fear of hitting our own chaps. There was a hell of a row from the starboard guns and momentarily distracted, it was some seconds before we realized that the plane banking round our bow and sweeping into a sharp turn towards us was a Jap Zeke Zero. Bright flashes from his wings meant that stuff was coming at us at point blank range. Nobody could have heard me as I yelled "Fire, Fire, Fire", but Rowson felt the flat of my hand on his back and immediately hunched up on to the back of his seat and crouched like a jockey, singing at the top of his voice, "How we gonna keep 'em down on the farm", to the rhythm of the gun. I watched his tracers as they ripped into the underbelly of the Zeke and could clearly see the pilot now as he roared only about 15 feet above our heads, dressed in green and yellow. A split second later there was no evidence that he had ever existed, although there was rumour that someone had found a piece of finger plus an arm. I suppose too, he had a mother who would never know that her son was the first kamikaze pilot to hit a British ship. But this was history, and we never noticed the blast as we selected our next target. I looked towards Arral but couldn't see him, so back I went up to the weather deck and looked down to see him lying in a bundle beside his gun. Thoughts of tourniquets and splints flashed through my mind and I was fearful of picking up a dead body.

As I bent over him, he stared through me and his lips trembled. He was alive and seemingly unhurt save for a trickle of blood near his eye. He tried to speak but couldn't, so I got him into a fireman's lift and climbed very slowly with him back on deck and into the nearest first aid post. In spite of the heat of the day, they placed a blanket around his shoulders and as I turned to go, I saw tears in his eyes. Oh God, what a war. I retraced my steps past the eight barrelled pom-pom or "Chicago Piano" and leaned over the rail to Rowson. "It's concussion or shell-shock I think, I expect he'll be all right – good shooting by the way, I'll go and take over his gun till I get relieved." Rowson grinned and hunched his shoulders in a long shrug. During a lull, Commander Whitfield asked on one of his rounds, "What are you doing there Eadon, where's the gunner?"

"He's at the first aid post, Sir."

"Right, I'll send a relief and when he arrives, get back to your post. Well done, keep your eyes skinned."

"Aye aye, sir."

And he was gone, booming words of reassurance and encouragement.

When I returned to Rowson, we went back to cruising stations and I climbed up on to a rail on the weather deck and peered across the flight deck. Where the base of the island structure had been, there was a bloody great hole and hooded firefighters were cleaning up the mess. The stanchion of the forward barrier had been destroyed. Signal lamps were flashing to and from the flag ship and some of our aircraft, now low on fuel, were diverting to other carriers. The buzz on deck was that we had 10 or 11 dead and about 20 wounded. We heard that a doctor and an air engineer officer had been killed by the suicide attack and also Sub Lt (A) W.G. Gileson who was in the Aircrew Room. When I learned that the engineer was my cabin mate Len, I took a deep breath, conscious that he no longer could. I laughed. I suppose it was a form of hysteria, because as I went down on the gun sponson my eyes filled and in cold anger I said to Rowson, "My cabin mate is dead, let's get the bastards".

I don't know whether we did or not, I just know that at that point fear left me, and the deafening rhythmic thumping roar of the Chicago Piano for'ard of us didn't bother me one bit. Our tracers glided into the sky like Roman candles or tennis balls. The "heavies" created clusters of white cloudlets where they exploded and the black expanding balls of smoke at sea level showed where our cross-fire had brought down another Jap. Though I seldom smoked cigarettes, I carried a cigarette case, which my father had given me, in my left breast pocket. It was a futile gesture to protect my heart, for a 20 mm cannon shell would have gone through it, and me, like a knife through soft marge. I thought of my grandparents, my parents, close relatives, friends and of course, my Rosamund. I knew that they had been going through it too back home, with long nights of bombing, and spasmodic mail only increased the concern.

Darkness fell like a final curtain, as the fleet altered course eastwards and I went back to my cabin. I locked the door and as I saw Len's shaving gear and his copy of *The Seven Pillars of Wisdom*, I sat down and wept. Then, devoid of emotion, I carefully packed his belongings into his cases and when done, I wrote a letter to his mother and father in Guildford, telling them how he had inspired me and listing the presents he had bought for them in Port Said and Ceylon. Four of my lads were killed: Thomas, Askew, Munro and Bainbridge.

There is an unusual sequel to this story. Truth is stranger than fiction it is said. Two years after my marriage to Rosamund she went to have her hair done one day when her mother and I were enjoying a cup of tea and a chat. She said, "Rosamund's looking better Stuart, she had a rough time you know." She had hardly mentioned her illness. "It was over two years ago you know", Ma continued, ". . . and she had been nursing for about nine months continuously on night duty. She came home from the pictures one evening and rang the door bell. Her sister answered the door and Rosamund said, 'Let me in, Georgie, I'm going to faint'. She came in and collapsed in the hall. We called the doctor because she was delirious and he diagnosed complete nervous exhaustion. She kept calling your name, so we put it down to worry. However, when she regained consciousness two days later, she told us she had seen you 'hanging over the side' of your ship. I don't know what she meant, but then she spoke some nonsense about white tennis balls floating into the sky, red flashes, white puffs of smoke in the sky and black puffs on the sea."

I was unaware of this although I knew she had collapsed and I had been worried because I did not get any letters for six weeks. She hadn't told me about the delirium. "When did this happen?" I asked, "When did she collapse?" Ma went through to the bedroom on the ground floor. She returned a few minutes later with a small diary and began to turn the pages. "It was Easter, yes I remember that. Oh here it is, Saturday evening." I still don't know what prompted me to ask, "What time, Ma?" Ma replied, "Oh I remember that because the 9 o'clock news was just starting."

I added ten hours to 9 o'clock p.m. and made it 7 o'clock a.m. So, allowing for the International Dateline, Rosamund had collapsed at precisely the moment we were hit by the Jap kamikaze. It was, and still is, incredible. The "tennis balls" of course were the tracers, the red flashes the guns, the white puffs the ack-ack shell bursts, the black puffs were the Jap aircraft exploding in the sea, and me "hanging over the side" of the ship, well that was the gun sponson.

Rosamund had "seen" it all – she had been there with me. She always will be with me and I with her.'

CHAPTER FIVE

'Some People Never Learn!'

TO ALL RANKS: 22 JUNE 1944

BRITISH TROOPS ADVANCING SOUTH FROM KOHIMA have today made contact with 4 Corps troop moving north from Imphal. This is a fitting time for me to express to all ranks my very high appreciation of your achievement in the long battle for Imphal – you have had to wait for two years, two years of hardship and strain, for this opportunity to inflict defeat upon the Japanese, but now that the opportunity has come, you have made full use of it. I expect very great things from 23 Division but your steadfastness, powers of endurance, your will to Victory and courage have surpassed all expectations. I am more proud than words can express of the honour of having been in command of you. You can also be supremely proud of the success you have achieved. For three months you have fought continuously, cut off for most of the time except by air, you have never wavered and have accepted – cheerfully, all hardships and privations, imbued solely with determination to defeat the enemy. The Japs have been and still are being defeated on all fronts – in Burma and the Pacific. On this front they have suffered enormous casualties and are demoralized and exhausted. We must make sure we gain the full fruits of our Victory. We must give them no respite but attack them and drive the scattered remnants from whence they came, right out of Burma. I thank you all for what you have achieved in the past.
LET US NOW GO ON TO VICTORY.

FROM: MAJOR-GENERAL O.L. ROBERTS CBE, DSO
COMMANDER 23rd INDIAN DIVISION

Bill Johnson
37 BRIGADE

Major-General Roberts spoke of a great victory, but 22 June was no Mafeking night for us as the general's words came to a division that had plenty on its hands. The 37 Brigade looked out into the cold wet night at Shenam, the RAJ–RIF were wrestling with Japs who had come through a gap up the Sengmai Turel, the Hyderabads and the 4th Mahrattas maintained lonely watches on the line of solitary peaks north of Turel. The Japs were on Lone Tree Hill and his forward troops were only 2 miles from Palel Bridge. The wind tore at the jungle and the rain was part of men's lives. There was no respite for those called on to complete the rout of the shattered remnants of the Japanese Imperial Armies, and so the Imphal siege almost passed unnoticed and that our turn was coming to march east.

JUNGLE NIGHT

The man with the green cigarette strolls down the path
Waving it in the air in conversation.
The man with the tiny anvil strikes it softly like a bell—
Tink-tink; tink-tink.
The man with the dark blue cloak goes quietly by.
There goes the man with the green cigarette again.

They are not really there. You know quite well
They are not there.
Then one of them whistles softly
You finger the trigger of your Bren.
Half-fearing, half-desiring the sudden hell
Pressure will loose.
You listen—
Nothing—
Then—

The man with the green cigarette strolls by again
Waving it in the air.
Down comes the dew,
Drip-drip; drip-drip.
The man with the tiny silver anvil
Strikes twice; strikes twice
Softly passes the man with the cloak of blue.

Fireflies.
Bell birds.
Shadows.
Japanese.

'K'
June 1945

Catherine Cleary
QA NURSE

It is so sad that little mention is made of the nursing personnel. I worked at 38
British General Hospital situated on the hillside of Imphal and also 66 Indian
General Hospital at Dimapur receiving the wounded from the Kohima battle site.
We nursing sisters were on the trains accompanying the wounded patients from
Dimapur railhead to the boat going across the Brahmaputra bound for Calcutta
hospitals and the forward Malarial Units No. 6 IMFTU. The troops staggered

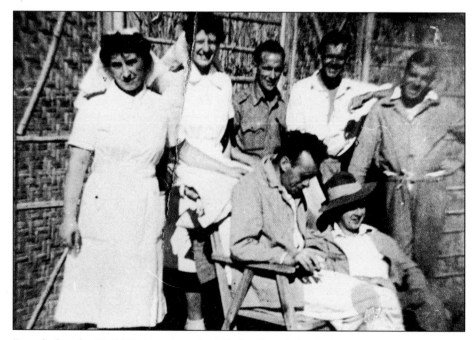

'I worked at the 38 BGH situated on the hillside of Imphal and also the 66 IGH at Dimapur,
receiving wounded from the Kohima battle site.'

into the tent hospital at a place called Gologath. I could not find it on the map, it was some place in SEAC pitched into tentage in a swamp paddy field.

My war diary reads as follows: 'Medical Parade today: 250 patients handed quinine, mepacrine and pamaquin, after blood tests – if they were negative, up the line went Tommy.' I could not have done the work without the marvellous Indian and British doctors constantly nursing with us five QAs.

The hospital at Panitola received the Chindits and Africans, flown in by the RAF and the USAAF; strange-looking men with beards, jungle sores, wounds, trench feet and exhaustion. They were a sad sight. The outstanding feature was their cheerfulness and good manners – all gentlemen. Major Kelly, a surgeon from the Indian Medical Service and Theatre Sister Molly Magee were magnificent. The operations went on in monsoon heat from one long day into night without a stop. On ending our tour of duty we five QAs returned to Imphal to nurse more casualties from across the Chindwin. General Slim visited the hospital on Christmas Day 1944; the patients and nurses enjoyed his visit and we sang carols for the patients and carried our lanterns round the wards.

The 38 British General Hospital was getting ready to go to Rangoon but I stayed at Chittagong. On New Year's Day 1945 a great noise was heard outside the sister's office. The REME's gift to the staff had arrived at 8 p.m. Four jeeps were outside with an officer in charge of three ducks dressed in neat uniforms, Army, Navy and Air Force – the little uniforms complete in every detail. Ducks were quacking all over the mess. Matron could not believe it and was cross at first, saying, 'Now, if this is all you lot have to do, it is no wonder we are not in Rangoon!' She was a wonderful lady and after a while joined in the fun. Each man was given a precious bottle from our ration store. Matron asked them to stay for dinner but they declined, saying, 'We are on our way to Rangoon – we'll meet you there!' I wonder if they did?

Jim R. Allen
2ND GREEN HOWARDS

Jim Allen was commissioned to the KOYLI regiment in 1940, and was later seconded to the 2nd Green Howards with whom he fought in the Arakan, Burma. Jim's patrol was ambushed; his spine was fractured when a Japanese soldier dropped on to him from a tree. A founder member of the Burma Star Association, his book *In The Trade of War* provides this extract.

These patrols were routine affairs usually reporting NES on their return, so I was perhaps a little careless. If I was I certainly paid the penalty and learned the hard way that it was never wise to take the Jap too lightly or underestimate his capacity for bouncing back to cause trouble. The patrol was about three hours out and I was, quite incorrectly, in second place and foolishly thinking of other things when suddenly all hell was let loose with the rattle of LMGs and then I felt a terrible blow on my upper back and I fell to the ground feeling winded and very, very frightened. I tried to rise but found somebody was holding me from behind and, despite the agonizing pain in my back, I managed to turn to discover a Japanese was struggling with me. He had a sword which he was trying to use while still grappling with me. I knew that I was literally fighting for my life and managed to draw the kukri that I always carried. Being much shorter than the sword I was able to use it to hack at the Jap's neck awkwardly with the kukri in my right hand while I held the sword off with my left. All this was – and still is – very vague to me and I think I was acting in primeval panic and instinct. I was aware of gunfire and shouts all round me as I continued to struggle automatically, and then there was no need as my opponent, whose smell still lingers in my nostrils, was no longer struggling but had gone limp.

'These patrols were routine affairs usually reporting NES (No Enemy Seen), on their return.' 2nd Green Howards approaching Ramree Island in January 1945.

AND SUNSET IN THE ARAKAN

When all these days of war are done
And we, beneath a kinder sun,
Look back and see the days we spent
In barracks, basha, trench and tent—
With calmer eye and heart at rest,
What shall we then remember best?

I know that I shall always see
The Ops Room where I used to be,
A jungle basha, map and plot,
The crew who worked throughout the hot
Long days and nights, and all the thrill
As Spitfires scrambled for the kill.

I shall recall each place and plain
From Akyab up the Kaladan,
The battle line that stretched along
The battered road to Buthidaung,
And then the unexpected boon

Japanese intelligence reports said British Beaufighter crews were brave men. Nicknamed 'Whispering Death' the Beaufighters of 177 Squadron put fear into Japanese hearts and minds.

Of film shows underneath the moon.
Or swimming in the tropic sea—
The sweating joy of mugs of tea.

There is so much we shall forget
That now is real to us, and yet,
As all the years go rolling by
And we beneath an English sky
Take up the task we left behind,
Go on in faith and hope to find
The world we fought to build, and see
A wider finer liberty.

We shall remember scenes and places
And half a hundred friendly faces,
The ways of war, the ways of man,
And sunset in the Arakan.

Kenneth Saville
March 1945

Corporal Jones, 2nd Green Howards, supervizes friendly Burmese building river rafts in the Arakan.

Edmund Horner
5070 AMES RAF

AMES was the cover for radar stations and stood for Air Ministry Experimental Station. Arriving in Bombay in 1943 I eventually turned up at Worli, then Silchar in Assam, then Chillong, Kohima, Imphal, Kalewa, Monywa and Meiktila. By the time the war had ended I had perforated eardrums. The RAF refused to fly me out as they said I did not have a parachute! So I hitched a lift out of Burma to Chittagong with an American pilot. Flying in a Dakota I arrived at Calcutta where I spent a fortnight in a British military hospital. From there I had the marvellous experience of being flown clear across India to Karachi in a Sunderland flying-boat.

The Dakota was a reliable aircraft but most uncomfortable, especially on my next journey to Aden. Everyone's kit was stacked down the centre of the fuselage and we sat hunched-up on small bench seats on either side. From Aden we again flew in a Dak to Lydda, Palestine, then another flight to Sardinia and the final leg across Europe to London.

Looking back on my days in Burma my outstanding memory is of coming across an abandoned Japanese camp with so many dead Japs lying everywhere –

'. . . I had the marvellous experience of being flown across India to Karachi in a Sunderland flying-boat.' The Ceylon-based Sunderlands receive a service by their maintenance crews.

many of them headless. I somehow lost my appetite. I managed to bring back as souvenirs a Japanese battle flag and a pair of canvas sniper boots.

Helen Hughes
FORCES HELP SOCIETY

After receiving my tropical kit and bedding roll at Bombay I set out for a place near Nagpur called Bilaspur. They gave me a flit-gun for use against livestock that might trouble me at night, but it was no protection against human livestock who tried to get into my carriage, so I locked myself in.

My duties were with an airborne division preparing to go into action. They were a marvellous bunch of men. One of these red beret soldiers said, 'So you are to be our "passionate lady" then?' 'Oh, no,' I replied, '"compassionate."' He had expected that I would arrange parties and dances and things. There was more serious work to be done on the welfare side because many men had all sorts of problems back home. I must have done a fair job because the general wanted to present me with the coveted red beret. Unfortunately, my boss thought otherwise and it was refused. But nearly fifty years later the veterans of this division bestowed a red beret upon me with great ceremony.

A Beaufighter of 177 Squadron, Chiringa, starting engines before setting off on a low-level strafing sortie over the enemy-held jungles of Burma in 1944.

W. Parker
RAOC 82nd WEST AFRICAN DIVISION

I arrived in Accra on the west coast of Africa and took over a platoon of West African and British troops. I was quite taken aback to discover that whatever their rank (even sergeant majors), the Africans had to take orders from a humble British private. It appears it had always been like that. We moved down the Gold Coast to Nigeria by road, where we trained for our job of providing vehicles, spare parts and weapons to the fighting troops.

We eventually came ashore at Karachi then made a three-day journey across the Sind Desert. There was a sandstorm en route which brought the train to a standstill. All doors and windows were shut tight but still the sand blew in, covering us and our equipment in a fine pumice-like dust. I managed to get one shave on that journey by scrounging hot water from the engine driver. At one stop white women were waiting to serve tea to the troops. It was a novel experience for our African friends and also, perhaps, for the tea ladies. We pitched camp at Ranchi, some 200 miles from Calcutta.

Lofty, who was 6 feet 7 inches tall with a high-pitched voice, frightened the life out of us once when he screamed, 'There's a scorpion in my bed!' Then, later, a huge green snake was silently gliding across the mess floor. We all started to yell and mill around jumping up on the tables in sheer panic. The orderly officer calmly walked in and chopped the snake in half with a huge machete – two portions, each over a yard long.

The African soldier was a cheerful man, perhaps out of his depth and slightly perplexed. After all, it was not his war. But, like us, they were not immune to death by accident or enemy action, nor were they immune from tropical diseases. They were likeable and willing learners, often weary with the war and, like us, overworked. Out of our complement of British Other Ranks only two stayed the course. The Hausa tribesmen tended to be on the tall side so they were usually picked to serve in the division's military police. At least they looked the part.

I shall never forget the British chap who came out as a replacement when we were erecting bashas in Prome. He had a glass eye. We all imagined the original had been lost in action somewhere. He was in charge of the Africans erecting these bashas so when he had to leave them for a while he took out his glass eye and put it in a box. He told the wild-eyed Africans that he was a juju man and would be keeping an eye on them while he was away!

Care of arms on active service was considered sacrosanct. Woe betide anyone who lost his weapon. One of the African sergeant majors went a little doolalli looking for his rifle. Eventually he found it in the latrine where he had paid a visit.

When we arrived at the pleasant island of Ramree the Japanese had gone. The

'The African soldier was a cheerful man, perhaps out of his depth and slightly perplexed. After all it was not his war.' Two African soldiers guard a Japanese POW.

villagers were friendly and we began waterproofing vehicles for an amphibious landing. Then I was informed I was going home on a month's leave (LIAP). Flown to Chittagong by Dakota the army decided to make me a PT instructor and guard commander. I hitched a lift to the airport then scrounged a ride on a Dakota warming up on the tarmac. I climbed on board and it flew to Calcutta. I guess they are still looking for me at that transit camp in Chittagong!

SANCTUARY

Is there some quiet place where I might hide
And rest my weary head a little while,
Some spot where sergeant-majors do not bide,
Still undiscovered by the rank and file?

O, is there such a place where I might pass
   An hour or two in idle solitude,
Away from life's mad melancholy farce,
   Far from the vast and vulgar multitude?

Yes, there is such a place within my ken
   Where I may rest and all my cares forget,
For wars and woes and worries vanish when
   I crawl beneath my old mosquito net.

Frolick
January 1945

Matt Nash
2ND BATTALION BLACK WATCH

In 1945 the jungle training camp for the 44th Indian Airborne Division was situated in the vicinity of the village of Bilaspur, Central Provinces. This was virgin jungle country with all the usual inhabitants you would expect to find in such a location: elephants, pythons and baboons, all big enough to avoid. It was the smaller and mainly insect life that proved most difficult to live with. On any morning, for a few minutes after reveille had sounded, a persistent banging noise in the company lines signalled the attempt by the soldiery to dislodge scorpions from their footwear by thumping their boots on the mud-packed floor of their bashas! The next major event of the day was waiting for the orderly sergeant to shoot or otherwise remove any snakes that were lurking in the cesspits that served as toilets.

Most of the day was spent avoiding bad-tempered sergeants and equally foul-tempered baboons. These particular animals, which lined the trees of any cleared space, reacted with interest to football games, which they seemed to approve of, or howled their contempt for any activity that disturbed them.

So the time passed in a constant awareness of nature until one morning someone noticed that between the rows of bashas, and set about 6 feet apart, were the unmistakable pug marks of a large tiger. The thought that during the night a tiger, later identified as male, had walked by within a few feet of your head in search of food was disturbing, to say the least.

At last we had found a reason to berate our 'gung ho' officers and chivvy them into a little action. After all, since they had arrived in the camp, their conversation had been about their skills as big white game hunters. They did respond to this call for action, on the grounds that no member of the company was going to sleep that night unless there were armed guards posted every few feet throughout the camp lines. And they formulated a plan. A goat was purchased from a local village and, with the assistance of the MT section, was tethered in the back of a small truck parked close to the jungle edge where the tiger had emerged.

Later that evening a number of the more nimble officers climbed the trees in the vicinity of the truck. Equipped with a formidable array of weapons, they settled down for the night in the hope that the tiger would appear. The night passed quietly – we know this for a fact; no one in the battalion was going to sleep with a big cat on the prowl.

In the early hours towards dawn our band of intrepid hunters climbed down from their trees. All that was found in the truck was a frayed end of rope – no goat! 'The goat must have chewed through the rope.' This and other explanations were offered, but none was to the satisfaction of the now growing crowd of weary soldiers, who could be heard muttering in the background such remarks as 'They were all bloody well fast asleep'.

Two weeks later, the tiger was spotted calmly drinking water from a nearby river. According to the observers, looking well fed and quite content!

Today Bilaspur is an important wildlife reserve, famed for its tigers and elephants.

Mike McCoy-Hill
INDIAN AIRBORNE

It was pitch dark when we detrained at Secunderabad. We were a sloppy lot from Deolali Transit Camp. Once off the train we were rounded up, very briskly, by a lot of NCOs in red berets, allocated to vehicles, and off we went into the night. To coin a phrase, our feet did not touch the ground. We knew instinctively that we had encountered a very different part of army life.

My recollections of Secunderabad seemed to be mainly bull . . . and assault courses, and a fatherly old bearer who was like a mother hen. At Bilaspur, quite apart from training, which seemed endless, it was the introduction to K rations and compo-packs. Those 'Camel to Consumer' cigarettes were something else. If you coughed while smoking them you were often left with an empty tube of paper! A bit of an overstatement, perhaps, but that dust-dry tobacco was not to be forgotten. I especially remember Rawalpindi for those huge 'punkas' in Napier Barracks, that creaked and groaned all night.

As to the jump training, it all went rather well, like oiled silk, except for one chap who I think was Wally Thompson. After one drop we all reported to the ground despatcher as normal when he called out our numbers – except for one.

To his number there was no reply. Then he was spotted, still up there. He had been carried into a thermal, drifted off, and eventually came down in scrub outside the dropping zone. Of course, we were told of the unfortunate Gurkha who got himself tangled up in his static lines, which had caught under his harness, and ended up flapping close to the tail wheel of the Dakota. He was made to jump again to qualify.

At Quetta, I remember, I always seemed to be humping coal sacks off lorries during fatigue duties. Those Afghan sheepskin coats we wore on night guard were warm – yes, but so stiff that it was almost impossible to get your rifle up to your shoulder.

I just did not like Quetta; it was cold and depressing. Then there was the Christmas dinner. The sergeant cook had at one time been employed in an up-market London hotel. He put on a marvellous spread which would not have been out of place at the Savoy. But so many blokes were drunk they couldn't eat it. The sweepers and sundry untouchables did very well. I don't think the cook ever forgave us.

'I recall the saga of the Indian Mutiny guns as if it was yesterday. They were found up-ended in the monsoon ditches on New Year's Day.'

I recall the saga of the Indian Mutiny guns as if it was yesterday. They were found up-ended in the monsoon ditches on New Year's Day!

There was a near riot at Karachi in a cinema following an incident when an Indian got his head thumped for not standing up when the National Anthem was played.

The Delhi Tattoo was not without incident either. Most of the blokes and guns went by train, but I was with the advance party sent by road to help set things up. It was a small convoy of jeeps with an LAD unit, travelling cross-country part of the way. What a way to see chunks of India, an adventure I would not have wanted to miss.

The celebrations were, to some extent, spoiled by rioting at the Red Fort, and a whole heap of 'Ghandi Wallahs' interfering with the parade. They chose to set about a Sherman tank, of all things. If they had chosen to set about us in our open jeeps things could have turned nasty. We had our rifles with us, of course, but we were not allowed ammunition. The only defence we had was drawn bayonets. These we sat on but showed no intent to use them. Frankly, I was glad eventually to get on the troopship *Devonshire* and sail for Palestine.

'There was a near riot at a Karachi cinema following an incident when an Indian got his head thumped for not standing up when the National Anthem was played.' The Paradise Cinema, Karachi.

Harold Russell
RAF REGIMENT

We were a small detachment guarding an airstrip close to the Bay of Bengal. There were just two tents and we did our own cooking, which proved both frustrating and amusing. Our brewing-up gear – tea, condensed milk and sugar – was stored in one tent, but no matter how well we sealed the sugar tins the hyenas always managed to open them and devour the contents.

Later, we went by LCT to Akyab Island where the heat was tremendous and half the world's fly population must have been living. It was disgusting not to be able to drink or eat without hundreds of them clinging around your face. Sunday 25 March 1945 saw our longest air raid so far. A fellow sergeant I had been with since 1941 was killed there.

We had a narrow squeak when our unit was guarding a stretch of the Irrawaddy River. We were very low on supplies so three of us set off, armed with only a couple of rifles and one revolver, to load up from a depot. We reached Nawin, and from then on drove past the startled faces of infantry who just stared at us from their foxholes beside the road. A mile further on we met a patrol who explained that the enemy were in force just up ahead. We reversed and got the hell out of there jildi!

Something not generally appreciated, perhaps, but we were conscious of the many benefits the British Forces brought to outlying villages. We used to make the rounds of villages nearby treating as many ailments as we could from our own medical stores. There were open sores, ulcers, ringworm and all sorts of things; there is no doubt in my mind that the villagers were grateful. They plied us with things like eggs and fruit in return for our services.

Arthur Driver
2ND BLACK WATCH

My first impression of India was exactly like the TV series *It 'Aint Half Hot, Mum*. Sleeping was made extra hot by having those ruddy mosquito nets – keeping out any cool breeze there might have been. Once we had just finished our sentry duty about midnight and were asleep in the guardroom, when in came the orderly officer accompanied by the orderly sergeant. I was put on a 'fizzer' for sleeping without my mosquito net. Reporting to the RSM (ex-Coldstream Guards) and the company commander (ex-Polish Airborne Brigade) next morning, I was subjected to a well-earned dressing down. 'Some people never learn', the RSM muttered, as I tripped over the doorstep, falling headlong into the office, my fellow defaulter cannoning into me and collapsing over me.

'Let's try again', said the RSM grimly. We wiped the smiles off our faces when we both received seven days' CB.

At Karachi I was put in hospital with acute peritonitis. Doing her daily rounds the matron spotted a red hackle on my tam-o'-shanter. For some reason she was not happy about it. 'Put it away in your locker', she snapped. The RAF patients wanted to know why she said this because their headgear was on their sidetables and she had raised no objection to them. I always carried a spare hackle in my wallet. One of the RAF 'erks' took this and placed it in a vase of flowers in the centre of the ward. It was the first thing matron saw when she made her next round. She was near to apoplexy and demanded its removal, and said that if it happened again she would put me on a 'fizzer'. Being confined to bed, I protested my innocence. But we never discovered the cause of her obvious aversion to red hackles, although we discovered she had been an army nurse!

Jim Smith
2ND INDEPENDENT PATHFINDER COY

Having been promoted to acting colour sergeant, taking over from the outgoing CQMS, I was landed with a problem. Men were complaining how our much-prized 'shirts Angola drab' that were so well made, were going missing at the dhobi at an alarming rate. I consulted the regimental provost sergeant, a fearsome man with bright ginger hair and handle-bar moustache. Between us we decided to carry out a raid on the dhobi-wallahs' tent when it became dark. There, we found our precious shirts hidden between layers of bedding on their charpoys.

We were, quite naturally, incensed and decided to take immediate action. All the dhobi-wallahs were bundled into a truck and carted off to a civilian police station where they were handed over to the dandi-wallahs. Back at the dhobi we faced the problem of sorting out the washed and unwashed clothes and of identifying each item by the names written on them in Hindi script. With 300 men this was nigh impossible. So it was back to the jail where we found the contractor who employed the dhobi-wallahs trying to bribe the dandi-wallahs to let his men go! We took them back to camp and made them sort out the clothes. There was no more pilfering after that, but it was some time before our chaps received their correct clothes back.

There was thick jungle on the edge of our camp at Bilaspur, jungle rumoured to conceal big game. We decided to become 'shikaris' and fifteen of us set off in extended line to beat the heavy undergrowth. It was not very long before we became separated. There were shouts from all directions. There was no wind to speak of and the clouds remained stationary. It was quite impossible to keep our bearings on what we could see through the trees and an hour later we were

'All the dhobi-wallahs were bundled into a truck and carted off to a civilian police station.'

completely lost. Someone scaled a tree to look for a landmark. It was close to sunset and we had no protection against mosquitos. We had neither food nor drink. Then someone else had the bright idea to fire off our rifles in Morse code – SOS – bang–bang–bang, bang–bang–bang, bang–bang–bang. We found a stream and followed it. This brought us to a river. By good fortune we heard the sound of a motor engine. A jeep full of sepoys was about to ford the river. We said we were lost. 'Apke paltan kiya hai sahib?' they asked, meaning, 'What is your unit?' Hanging my head in shame, I replied, 'Pathfinder Company'.

J.F. Warren
KOYLI

We disembarked at Bombay from the troopship *Nea Helos*, a Greek vessel which we had soon renamed the *Hell Ship*. The fresh water tanks hadn't been cleaned out for years as the water was black. Together with over three hundred lads, I was housed in a hold in the stern, immediately over the propellers. The floor area would have been sufficient for a one-bedroomed flat. We slept in three layers, one lot on the floor, another on the tables while the third were in hammocks suspended on hooks from the ceiling.

We were taken by train to a base reinforcement camp at Kalyan. Once there we were sorted out to join various battalions across India. With 600 others I was sent to New Delhi to join the 2nd Battalion, King's Own Yorkshire Light Infantry. This particular battalion had been reduced to only sixty-five men through the fighting in Burma in 1942. The remnants had been allocated internal security duties in the Delhi area, because a section of the Indian population was trying to sabotage the war effort in order to help the Japanese. Railways were disrupted by levering the track out of line, damaging points and signalling equipment.

In New Delhi we were housed in an old barracks used before the war by regular soldiers. There was a need to rebuild the battalion from scratch and so we were asked to fill in a questionnaire, which included some general knowledge questions, and asked for our preference to join HQ or rifle company duties. With usual army logic I was picked out for a 3 in mortar platoon after expressing my wish to be a signaller.

The specialized training coupled with battalion training took us up to April 1945, when it was decided to move south to Kola. From Kola we moved even further south into the middle of the Mysore jungle. Here we trained in jungle fighting with a view to joining the 14th Army in Burma on 1 September 1945. The monsoon had started and sleeping on groundsheets huddled in a monsoon cape was the normal experience for a couple of weeks until we could erect some bashas. There was plenty of bamboo growing nearby, some over 30 feet high and at least 1 foot in diameter at its base. Bamboo was most useful for a variety of jobs. It can be used as support poles or split open to make panels or halved in sections to make bowls or mugs. We made our huts with bunk-beds inside and canvas tent tops for a roof. Digging latrines and building stores kept us busy, working from dawn to dusk. A river close by, high with monsoon water and a deep brown colour, was our supply for drinking, washing and cooking. Making tea over an open wood fire in a galvanized steel bath full of brown water often prompted the question, 'Have you put the tea in, Bert?'

Although we had joined a Yorkshire regiment, about half the men were from the Midlands, either from Birmingham or Coventry. We never got as far as joining the 14th Army because the atom bombs were dropped on Japan. So we moved back to Kola where I developed malaria. I was flat on my back for about ten days and then on the eleventh day, with the usual army sympathy, was elected to do a twenty-four hour guard duty.

Of course, the end of the Second World War was not the end of the conflict. People living in colonies in various parts of the world were suddenly finding the confidence to throw off the shackles of their masters. We were told of a move to Lalitpur in Jhansi Province to carry out further training to enable us eventually to help the Dutch suppress a liberation movement in the Dutch East Indies (now Indonesia).

Before leaving Kola, however, I experienced one of the lasting impressions of India – the contrast between wealth and poverty. There were three of us on escort duty travelling by train, and on the way back we slept in a station waiting room. We visited the Mysore Palace and managed to see the Maharajah's coach houses. There were 154 coaches – one made of solid silver, and most of them were made in the UK. The harness rooms must have taken up half an acre and the total value of everything we saw was inestimable. On returning from our visit we were approached by a disabled child begging for half an anna. The population of India at that time was about 320 million with around 20 million living in absolute poverty.

Our intended deployment to the Dutch East Indies was cancelled, but we remained at Lalitpur until December 1946, before moving to Deolali in the Bombay plain. Humidity there was stifling – even the sweat of our bodies did not evaporate, it just ran down into our socks.

The Apollo Bundur, better known as the Gateway to India, was designed by Edwin Landseer Lutyens and erected at Bombay for the visit of King George V and Queen Mary in 1911.

Towards the end of October 1947, I remember standing on the deck of the troopship *Empress of Scotland*, watching the Taj Hotel and the famous 'Gateway to India' recede into the distance. I was homeward bound after three years in the sub-continent – and not a day too soon.

R.T. Davis
SERGEANT 122 LOC COMPANY INDIAN CORPS OF MILITARY POLICE

A big cheer went up when we docked at Bombay. We collected mosquito nets and were taken to a transit camp where we relaxed for two days giving us an opportunity to explore the city. It was fascinating but we were not impressed with the Indians constantly spitting out betel juice, their clothes – or lack of them – and the sight of so many sacred cows walking the dusty streets and through the markets. It was here we discovered the infamous kite hawk. They had no fear of man but their eagle-like appearance and wingspan of 4 or 5 feet were quite frightening.

Six days later we were on our way to Madras by train. Six of us were allocated to each compartment – one slept on each luggage rack, one on each wooden

'. . . we soon realized the compartment was infested with large ants, bugs and other insects.' RAF personnel en route from Secunderabad to Basal by 'de luxe' trooptrain.

slatted seat and two on the floor. We changed places each night. But we soon realized the compartment was infested with large ants, bugs and other insects. A wood-burning train pulled us about 100 miles each day, frequently stopping at small halts to take on wood fuel. It was then we made tea and collected a pack of food. Each carriage received one loaf of bread, and the only way to keep the ants at bay was to suspend it from the ceiling by string.

After staying at a tented transit camp just on the outskirts of Madras, we were loaded on to trucks with a supply of water in goat skins hanging from the radiators. The three-day journey – slow, bumpy and tremendously boring – was not made any the more cheerful by our being underfed, overheated and suffering from sore bottoms.

We arrived at Coimbatore. About 3 miles out of town we came to our military police camp, a collection of bashas – huts with straw roofs, straw walls, and a few openings round the walls with a cover propped up with sticks. These we let down in the evenings to keep out the flies, mosquitos and any other flying insects. This was to be our home for some months, situated in the middle of a desert which stretched for miles to some distant hills.

Our orderly room with a small basha adjoining for the OC was bare except for a few wooden crates. We set up shop. Bill had one large crate as a table and Harold and I shared the other with small boxes on which to sit. Our two officers had a desk of sorts and chairs which had seen better days. Somehow we managed to get some semblance of order into our primitive office. There were a few reams of poor-quality paper, a small packet of carbon paper, and some boxes of thorns for use as pins. We unloaded our sundry military impedimenta and were ready for action!

There was no electricity and each basha was issued with a Tilley lamp. When working correctly they gave out a very good light, the only trouble was obtaining new mantles which were like gold dust. Our cook found the cooking arrangements quite primitive as his field kitchen equipment worked on oil and water. Bare-boarded tables seating eight was our welcome in the dining-room, which doubled as an 'all ranks' mess for recreation.

Simpson, Harold and I slept in the orderly room. Our beds were wooden frames with thick rope stretched across; the mattress was usually two blankets laid over the ropes. At each corner was a long pole about 5 feet high which supported the mosquito net. Bugs were there in their thousands and we stopped them getting into our beds by placing the legs of each bed in a small tin of paraffin oil.

In this desolate desert of a place, of the many trials we had to endure the worst experience was when we heard of an epidemic of bubonic plague in a nearby village. As a safeguard everyone in 142 Unit – without exception – had to be inoculated. A doctor and one assistant set up a make-shift surgery and the only thing that made it look authentic was the white jackets they wore. During my time in the army I had been inoculated against just about everything known to man, but I had never before seen so large a syringe as those displayed. We were all inoculated with what appeared to be about half a pint of anti-bubonic serum. It was not an enjoyable experience, and out of the 142 men, all except 15 were required to repeat the performance!

When we arrived in India our unit had been in first-class shape, but after just a few months at Coimbatore many of the cheerful and quite healthy soldiers were lapsing into periods of melancholy. The long days and nights of intense heat, the barren desert and sand, the flies, mosquitos and complete lack of any interesting activity, caused many to think about home, their wives and children, or sweethearts they had left behind.

Any news of the outside world came to us through a small battery radio which our friend Milarick had begged, borrowed or possibly stolen, from the depot some 10 miles away. When would the war end? We waited for the great news to reach us – eventually.

Edgar Poole
SOMERSET LIGHT INFANTRY

A somewhat depleted 5th Battalion Somerset Light Infantry was pulled out of Burma to undertake the equally demanding job of service on the North West Frontier. I joined them at Peshawar as a warrant officer with experience but pink knees, having just arrived from Blighty. The CO already knew me and had decided to put A Company in my grasp. They were a motley collection of uncivilized, undisciplined men, few of whom were from Somerset. I thought they were an absolute shower. In the event, having been given a free hand, we soon had one of the smartest companies in the battalion, with a good reputation for sports and athletics.

When I came out of hospital after a close shave with diphtheria, I could have opted to take a cushy job, but at that stage the unit was assembled in a jungle ready to go back into action. Fortunately, the atom bombs were dropped. Many of us owe our lives to that event.

On our first day in India, however, marching from Deolali railway station to the transit camp, one of the draft dropped down dead with heat exhaustion. So our first duty in this God forsaken sub-continent was to form a burial party complete with a squad to fire volleys over the poor unfortunate's grave. To make things worse, the sergeant in charge was soon in trouble for not picking up the empty cartridge cases which had fallen into the open grave!

Deolali Camp was grim. The permanent staff warrant officer had a tent all to himself. When the monsoon came, mysteriously the huge stakes securing the guy ropes to his tent suddenly collapsed. It had nothing to do with the Somerset Light Infantry.

We always passed the Sikh barracks when on our route marches out of Peshawar. The Sikhs were not allowed to cut their hair or beards, and often we saw the sepoys with their hair grown down to their ankles. Our lads used to give a chorus of wolf-whistles, before passing through the gate of the mud-walled city and out into the dusty, glaring heat.

When firing live mortars up in the mountains we always followed the recognized drill if a bomb failed to explode. A careful watch was kept where the dud had landed. We then went out with detonators to carry out a controlled explosion. But the snag was that by the time we had got organized the Pathans had usually spirited the dud away. It was not a wise thing to do as one of our CSMs found out to his cost. He kept a dud on his desk for some time until it rolled off one day. When he went to pick it up – BANG!

On my last Christmas with the battalion the Maharajah of Dahtia State arrived with beaters and guns. He invited some of us to join him in a 'shikari' to hunt pheasant, wild boar and venison. I enjoyed the change of diet but always felt the disparity between the starving poor of India and the rich potentates. Even so, the Maharajah was a most pleasant fellow. When in charge of the party going home, he and his retinue were at a siding waiting to join our Bombay-bound train. His special carriage was coupled up to ours so that we could walk through. Perhaps he recognized that the days of the British Raj were nearly over.

Reginald Foster
REPORTER SEAC NEWS

During the Second World War not every army had its morning newspaper delivered by air! Thousands of service people in Burma did – flung by the bundle from a low-flying Anson aircraft, an RAF NCO at the door 'delivering' them in double-quick time while I checked the next batch to be dropped.

The 14th Army may have been the 'Forgotten Army' back home, but its very own newspaper remembered it. The paper was the brainchild of SEAC supremo Lord Louis Mountbatten and the editor was Frank Owen, a reporter famed as a great enemy of red tape and bureaucracy. I was certainly proud to be on his staff.

The paper was a lifeline between Burma and Blighty and between units themselves, even though one 'mob' might think another was getting too much publicity and credit in the fighting.

War correspendent Reginald Foster (right) with army photographer Fred Wackett (left), with warriors of the Maharajah of Manipur's élite bodyguard.

By way of contrast I covered a bizarre assignment in Manipur State which lies between Burma and Assam. It was the Maharajah's coronation and a scene straight from the tales of the Orient. The chief mantri, in flowing black robes, supervised the dressing of kneeling elephants with rich draperies and peacock-tailed canopies. There was an unending procession to propitiate the sacred snake, with wrestlers, dancers and musicians. The Maharajah spent three hours performing the religious part of the coronation alone and the whole event took twelve days to complete!

Flight Sergeant T.E. White, CGM
357 SQUADRON RAF

I served as an RAF parachute training instructor at Ringway, Manchester, in 1942 before being posted to Chaklala, India. By the end of my service I had completed 245 descents and was awarded a Mention in Despatches, and the CGM.

At Chaklala I was attached to 357 Special Duties Squadron, based at Dum Dum, where operations included dropping men and supplies to the insurgent groups behind the Japanese lines. On 14 March 1944, a Hudson took off at 2330 hrs to fly a supply dropping sorties; three hours later a signal was received by the squadron indicating that the Hudson had crashed. Four of the crew had been killed and two seriously injured. A doctor was urgently requested.

The squadron medical officer, Flight Lieutenant G.D. Graham MBE, immediately volunteered to parachute into the crash area. The pilot for the drop was Flight Lieutenant J.A. King DFC, who had already flown over that area the previous night. I also volunteered to accompany the doctor and assist in identifying and burying the dead airmen.

The drop took effect on 17 March, and soon after making a safe landing we learned that one of the injured men had since died of his wounds. We were met on the ground by Kokang guerillas dressed in blue uniforms and under the command of Colonel Yang Yan Sang. Mules were provided to carry our equipment for the one hour journey to the crash site near the village of Po Ko.

At a mountain hut we discovered the aircraft's navigator Flying Officer Prosser, the sole survivor of the crash. He had received rudimentary first aid administered by Major Leitch and Lieutenant Parsons of the American forces in the area. Prosser was feverish due to infection setting in on his wounds. He had suffered a fractured skull, cuts to his face and a fractured right ankle.

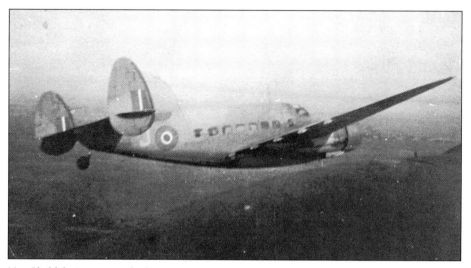

'At Chaklala I was attached to 357 Special Duties Squadron, based at Dum Dum, where operations included dropping men and supplies to the insurgent groups behind enemy lines.'

After the initial treatment Prosser improved slightly but, despite constant round-the-clock attendance, he suffered a relapse. An American doctor, Captain Hockman, arrived after a five-day journey by mule from the T Etang, and both he and Graham tended the ailing navigator.

Soon after the dead crewmen had been buried with full military honours, a signal was received indicating a strong Japanese force was heading in our direction – a mere four hours' march away. Further signals giving the enemy's movements were received with some misgivings. The enemy were now even closer and said to number over four hundred!

On 1 April it was decided to move into China. Prosser was carried on a litter by a dozen coolies who, during the night of 8 April, actually absconded from the party. I was sent on ahead to recruit new coolies and we managed to set off again the following day.

Two days later we were climbing a pass at 7,000 feet. A signal was sent back to the squadron and the very next day we were met by a weapon's carrier, which took us to 22 Field Hospital at Yunshin. An aircraft of American Transport Command flew us out to India on 17 April. We had covered over 100 miles in five days, over the most difficult terrain, while attending to our patient the whole time. Our mission of mercy had taken thirty-three days.

Tom Brookes
215 SQUADRON RAF

Taken from the Initial Training Wing at Cambridge in October 1942, I was put on a boat called *Laargs Bay*, which had been hastily converted into a troop transport, and we sailed for Durban, South Africa. Unfortunately, we were chased by German submarines and ended up in Bahia in South America, short of fuel and water. However, two months after leaving Bristol, I recommenced my training course in Southern Rhodesia.

The proud day came when I received my wings and moved for further training in Palestine, and then on to India by Sunderland flying-boat. At my heavy conversion course on to Liberators I picked up my crew of nine, which included a chap I had been at school with. All ten of us were non-commissioned. Our navigator was the eldest at twenty-one, being just a few months older than myself; the others were only just in their twenties.

We were posted to 215 Squadron in July 1944 and most of our operations involved seeking out Japanese locomotives on the Burma–Siam Railway. These locos were mainly used at night and hidden during the day inside large bamboo huts built over the railway line. One that we managed to find was located in a long narrow valley and in order to attack it we had to fly down the valley at very low

'One that we managed to find was located in a narrow valley and in order to attack it we had to fly down the valley at very low level strafing it with our .5 Brownings.'

level strafing it with our .5 Brownings. The Japs meanwhile had placed a machine-gun nest into the side of the hill overlooking the loco sheds and, not being able to see it, we were very surprised when bullets started raining down on us. Unfortunately, our waist gunner was hit in the ankle, knee and thigh of one leg, but we got him back to base. He was later tragically killed during a practice flight.

During this tour of 300 hours flying operations, the crew and I, complete with aeroplane, were seconded to the American Air Force. They needed some experimental bombing done for which the Liberators could be used. Incidentally, when we first landed at the American base we were guided to our dispersal area by a crew chief in a jeep. We all piled out of the B24 and the chief looked at us and our rank on our sleeves and asked, 'Who's the Goddamm skipper of this plane?' I said, 'Me,' and he said 'Jeez! What rank are you?'

The experimental bombs consisted of 50 gallon oil drums into which detonators had been inserted at one end and a crude tail fin fitted to the other. They were tied to our bomb racks with rope and, much to our horror when released, they were clanking together on their way down. Fortunately, they did not explode until they reached the ground where they went off with a blinding sheet of flame. We must have been some of the first planes to ever drop Napalm (this was done in complete ignorance of its effect – believe you me!)

'. . . the gun turrets were removed and belly tanks fitted in the bomb bays. We used to stagger into the air and fly over the Himalayas to China, off load, and return empty.'

Our tour completed, most of the crew left to become instructors. The remainder, including my wireless operator and navigator, stayed with me on the squadron and we completed another tour on Dakota transport aircraft without the usual three-months' rest period from operations. This tour was mainly supply dropping to the 14th Army and some of the airstrips were quite hazardous. It was especially difficult to find our destinations during the monsoon weather.

When this particular tour was over, I was posted back on to a Liberator converted to a tanker. This meant the gun turrets were removed and belly tanks were fitted in the bomb bays. We used to be filled up with petrol, stagger into the air and fly over the Himalayas into Kunming in the province of Yunnan, China, off load and return empty.

These trips were called Hump runs, and after completing forty-two of them my RAF career abroad came to an end. I eventually flew home, wiser and in some respects sadder because I had to leave my crew behind, especially my navigator and wireless operator. They had been with me during the training days, on to Libs and Daks and through two tours of operations and on all the Hump runs.

So what does the Burma Star mean to me? It means trying to find an airstrip on Akyab Island during the monsoon rains. It means flying over the Himalayas

P47 Thunderbolts of 30 Squadron prepare to take off from Feni in April 1944 to strafe Japanese supply lines and troop installations.

when the sun is setting. It means doing a radio let-down over Kunming in dense cloud, circling the airfield in a petrol-laden aircraft while other aircraft were in the vicinity. And, finally, it means having the responsibility of taking ten blokes across the Indian Ocean to the target and bringing them back safely, not once but many times.

Reg Child
RN COMMANDO

We landed on Gold Beach, Normandy, on D-Day and as soon as the fighting stopped in that area I volunteered for the Burma campaign! Transferred to No. 5 Commando I received my tropical jabs and without any embarkation leave found myself on a Dutch ship, the *Sibajaek*, and bound for Bombay.

Our jungle training on arrival was specially planned fo fit us for landings in swampy areas. We used rolls of ordinary chicken wire stiffened with bamboo canes with hessian backing sewn on. This was unrolled in front of us as we advanced into swamps. But you had to be quick before the 'carpet' sank into the mud. Successive parties would come up behind and lay more of this carpeting to approach enemy positions.

We carried out quite a few landings – Ramree Island, Rangoon, and Penang. Then we had a nice spell in Ootacamund ('Ooty' as it was known), before being taken back to Blighty on a hell ship called the *City of London*. Because of bad weather we put in at Casablanca for repairs and some of the soldiers, who had been in Burma for years and had been injured on the boat during the storm, actually went absent.

D. Moore
22 SQUADRON RAF

In January 1942 we were posted to Singapore – or so we believed, but when Singapore surrendered to the Japanese our troopship was diverted to Ceylon. Colombo had just received its first air raid. Our unit was sent from one jungle airstrip to another and we eventually found ourselves in a remote area on the border district of Burma. We scrounged an old mobile generator from the army and repaired it so that we could supply electric lighting to all our huts and bashas.

Lack of any form of entertainment was a problem we solved by building our very own radio station. We called it Radio NBG – (No Bloody Good). Everyone chipped in to help and before long the equipment and all the huts were wired-up to the central 'studio'. In spite of our name our programmes were pretty good and consisted of news bulletins from London, recordings of *ENSA* shows, shows we devised ourselves and of course record requests.

We built up quite a large library of record discs. Each time the squadron moved, however, it was fraught with difficulties when we were obliged to pack everything carefuly to avoid breakages. When the atom bombs dropped on Japan our radio equipment was eventually installed in a military hospital at *Poona*. Until then we had believed Poona was just a music hall joke, used by the comedians of the day. We soon found out it was a very large place with an army training barracks.

Ken Orton
1ST BATTALION SOUTH STAFFORDSHIRE REGIMENT

I started the war as a wireless op/air gunner but a nasty plane crash made me unfit for that job. I was transferred to the infantry! Recently I attended a spiritualist meeting where the medium asked me how long had I been in Africa. I replied truthfully, 'About two minutes'. You see, I had swum ashore at Port Said when shore leave was refused. I swam back again to the troopship before the red caps caught me.

In India we had to stand guard at the famous Red Fort. Next door to the armoury was the so-called unit library, a few books, two chairs and a dilapidated sofa, on which we used to sleep between spells on guard. Before long, however, Daily Routine Orders dictated, 'Guard personnel will NOT sleep on the library sofa'. Coming off guard duty one night I made arrangements to sleep on the floor. Then in came a pi-dog, the type that seem to haunt India, climbed up on to the sofa and went to sleep. My first thought was to kick him out, but then I thought 'Oh, what the hell!'

I can understand where the term 'doolally tap' came from. At the Deolali Transit Camp, hundreds of soldiers of all ranks used to stand on a box every day and yell out their names and numbers. These were the men destined for the next troopship home. Everyone developed a nervous tic, which would curiously disappear soon after they had embarked safely aboard and watched the Gateway of India at Bombay docks receding into the distance.

Beaufighters of 177 Squadron, based at Chiringa, attack a Japanese coastal vessel near Rangoon in May 1944.

Fred Farrall
978 BALLOON SQUADRON RAF

I joined the RAF in February 1939, and a year later was with a balloon unit in Scotland. The RAF balloon units destined for India/Burma, left the UK in February 1942 and I was one of the personnel. Balloons were flown by 978 Squadron around Calcutta, while those of 979 Squadron served the Tata Works Complex in Jamshedpur, some 200 miles north-west of Calcutta.

For some time the No. 2 Mobile Balloon Flight served an American air base at Kharagpur from where supplies, including fuel, were flown to China. Eventually we were transferred to Burma by Dakota aircraft, then moved by road to Kalewa on the Chindwin River. It was 10 December 1944 that Indian sappers and miners completed the largest Bailey bridge ever built – over 1,154 feet long. The spans were assembled under cover in the Myittha River, then floated down in sections in to the Chindwin and fixed together in just twenty-eight hours. It was a commendable piece of engineering. Being exposed to air attack our balloon flight was moved into position around the bridge.

'At the Chindwin River we flew five balloons over the bridge and later we were sent to the Irrawaddy River, north of Mandalay, where our unit acted as decoys.'

The personnel of No. 2 Mobile Balloon Flight had already been on an assault course at Kharakvasla near Poona – a tough course for young RAF lads, and we were eventually transferred to a similar course just outside Bombay. Together with army and naval units we trained on sea-going craft as part of Combined Operations to make an assault on the Addaman Islands, but the whole operation was cancelled.

At the Chindwin River site we flew five balloons over the bridge and later were sent to the Irrawaddy River north of Mandalay, where our unit acted as decoys. To our surprise and apprehension, army and navy units were using dummy equipment. At the time, Japanese river craft were plying up and down the river each evening to obtain supplies from a rice dump. It was a frightening experience, I can tell you. We watched them but we were under strict orders not to take any action.

No. 2 Mobile Balloon Flight was disbanded about April 1945, being sent back to Calcutta by road and rail. I eventually flew home in a converted Liberator bomber, a journey which took a whole month to complete, stopping five or more times in different countries – not a comfortable trip, I must say. I was demobbed on 4 April 1946, having served seven years in the RAF, four of them in India and Burma.

Ted Parsons
884 WATER TRANSPORT COMPANY RASC

Messing about in boats especially appealed to me. We trained on various boats from open launches, ships' lifeboats, cabin cruisers and a steam yacht, and even a Norwegian trawler. At the time we were in Scotland where it was bitterly cold. V2 rockets were falling on London when we embarked on the P & O liner *Stratheden*, en route for Bombay.

At Kalyan our kit was dyed jungle green and then we hung about until the middle of the night to board a train. It arrived seven hours later, and the journey took seven days, stopping and starting, backing into sidings and surrounded by Indians selling just about everything. One of them was calling out, 'Bow leg wallah – bow leg wallah!' I looked at his legs and they were as straight as mine. Then I twigged – he was calling out, 'Boiled egg, wallah!'

From Calcutta we flew to Burma – twice, as the first aircraft developed an engine fault. Our camp at Chittagong was formerly a rice paddy field and was under water. So we billeted in an abandoned convent in the town. Piled into jeeps we went to Kalewa on the Chindwin River to live under canvas. The Japanese had been pushed back by then and soon Mandalay was recaptured. With Burmese as our labour force we assembled 30 foot steel river boats which

'At the time, Japanese river craft were plying up and down the river each evening to obtain their rice supplies from a dump.'

arrived in sections and were put together like a kit. They were extremely basic in design with no cover or galley but possessing two diesel engines. The galley, if you can call it that, was a Bengazi cooker at the stern, in reality a tin full of sand soaked in petrol used for a stove.

The river was uncharted. On the first day of a 250 mile trip to reach a supply dump on the Irrawaddy, towing two steel barges we went aground on a sandbank. It took one and a half days to get off. Then the rains came. We set off on another journey with a barge on either side of us. The return journey took nearly six weeks. By then the river had swollen some 20 feet higher due to the monsoon water, and it was getting closer to our tented camp.

Petrol was transported by river. We made rafts by lashing together a huge number of 50 gallon drums, decked over with bamboo and we even made a tiny cabin at the stern with the same material. The rafts were quite stable, even on a fast-flowing river.

We came out of Burma after VE-Day. Being a water-borne unit we had no motor transport and were constantly going cap-in-hand to various other units to scrounge some. The tracks used as roads were in a poor state and progress was slow. Chopping trees down en route to repair the tracks made life even more difficult. All the time we lived on bare rations. We were sick and tired of the tins of M & V (meat and vegetables) nicknamed 'Maconachies' after the manufacturer.

Back at Calcutta we were billeted in a small block of flats in Heysham Road in the Indian quarter of the city. The climate was so hot and humid that we suffered with prickly heat, and the flats were alive with bedbugs. The dhobi-wallah next door used to lay out our washing on the river bank where the cattle used to lay. Consequently we soon had ringworm.

For a short time I lived on one of the vessels. All humanity was there. Hundreds of Indians would come to bathe in the foul water. The less fortunate would float by having departed this life and having been partially cremated by their families.

The invasion of Malaya, Operation 'Zipper', was now being prepared. We set about camouflaging our launches moored in the Doppa Lock. To get there each day we were driven through a heavily populated part of the city. It was a scene of utter squalor – dung cakes out to dry on the mud-built houses, open-fronted shops, smoke rising from a million little fires in earthenware ovens, traders of all kinds carrying goods on their heads, on their backs or suspended from yokes laying across their shoulders. We became used to the sight of the hundreds of street beggars and vendors. And then we saw the glue factory.

It was a one-storey timber and corrugated building with piles of cattle feet and lower limbs waiting for the boiling pot. The smell was vile and no words of mine can adequately describe it. The crowning glory of this ghastly scene was the row upon row of vultures, rubbing shoulders with each other on the roof, eyeing the animal remains with relish.

Work finished at noon, when it was time for the traditional siesta known as 'charpoy drill'. After tea and a shower we usually visited Chowringhee. This was a square mile of the city given over to the entertainment provided by cinemas, bars and restaurants. One frequented by BORs was Firpos Restaurant. It was a clean and luxurious edifice, the waiters in crisp white uniforms with brightly coloured turbans, electric punkahs, ice-cold Tiger beer. There were wild celebrations here for VJ-Day.

'. . . one of them used was the Firpos Restaurant. It was a clean and luxurious edifice, the waiters in crisp white uniforms with brightly coloured turbans.'

Walter Barnard
RAF

I left the Heavy Glider Conversion Unit at North Luffenham in September 1944. We had been helping in the training of the 6th Airborne Division in their task of learning to fly the Horsa glider, and soon after D-Day was over I found myself on the troopship *Athlone Castle*, destined for India.

After two weeks in Bombay where I swopped my 'Bombay Bowler', which looked like a left-over from the Victorian era, for a bush hat, I left on a train with five other sergeants for our first posting. This was an RAF airfield at Salawas, about 15 miles from the town of Jodhpur in Rajasthan. The water supply came from Jodhpur in an open ditch and on reaching the camp went through a chlorination plant, with the result that it had the appearance of diluted milk when poured into a glass.

Jodhpur is situated on the fringe of the Thar Desert and peak summer temperatures were about 120 degrees in the shade. In the winter mornings we

An American Superfortress lands at Chiringa out of fuel. When the pilot saw the little petrol bowser approach he remarked, 'Geez! I want petrol for my plane not my lighter!'

paraded in greatcoats, but by midday the temperature would have reached about 60 degrees. In the hot season, however, only urgent work was carried out after tiffin. We were a maintenance unit and serviced all types of aircraft, but mainly the American Liberator bombers which were used extensively for the Burma campaign. Working under the Perspex cockpit canopy in the hot sun, the temperature would have exceeded the shade temperature of 120 degrees. About half an hour in the aircraft was more than enough!

Christmas 1944 was an unforgettable experience. We received an invitation along with all the personnel at RAF Jodhpur to attend a Christmas party at the palace of the Maharajah of Jodhpur. Truckload after truckload of airmen and officers – there must have been over a thousand in all – arrived at the front entrance to the palace. There on the steps of the magnificent doorway stood the Maharajah himself, Umaid Singh, and he shook hands with everyone as they went in. As we entered we were each given chits entitling us to so many tots of spirit and so many bottles of beer. A large hall off the central area had been set down the middle with trestle tables each seating about a dozen men, while all around the sides of the hall other tables were arranged behind which stood servants of the Maharajah. On these tables were the footstuffs to be given out to the men – and what a spread there was after what we had been used to! An

ENSA party had come from Delhi to entertain and there were various other diversions, even a film show in the Maharajah's private cinema. The whole affair concluded the next morning with breakfast at about eight o'clock, and then it was back to camp.

How the opulence of the surroundings contrasted with the poverty to be found outside in the city, where cattle roamed the streets, and that ever prevalent heavy scent filled the air in the hot atmosphere.

I had the misfortune to contract dysentery and was sent to the hospital at Jodhpur. While there I met another airman who was from Salawas and had been injured in an aircraft accident. He had been in a Liberator on an air test, and on descending the pilot was unable to level out. The bomber simply came down until it ploughed into the ground out in the desert.

A few days before the monsoon arrived, the evenings became chilly and breezy. In the darkness across the desert the sky would be lit by flashes of lightning of so many different colours, red and orange and green, and the rising wind brought millions of all kinds of insects – as if we hadn't got enough already! Then it rained. And how we enjoyed it, standing out in it and getting soaked to the skin after all the months of getting parched in the sun. I suppose we stood it all rather stoically, knowing that there was a job to be done.

'. . . another airman from Salawas was injured when his Liberator, on test flight, simply came down until it ploughed into the desert.'

'I suppose we stood it all rather stoically knowing that there was a job to be done . . . the time began to drag as each of us waited for our demob number to come closer.'

With the advent of VE-Day on the day after I was twenty-one years old – what a birthday present – and then VJ-Day, the time began to drag as each of us waited for our demob number to come closer and our return to England made certain.

In retrospect, there was a memorable conclusion to my stint in India. I was sent home on compassionate grounds and was flown out by one of the old flying-boats in what must have been posh inter-war years' style – via Karachi, Bahrain, Cairo, Marseille, Poole Harbour, then a coach to London, a hop on the Underground and indoors at Tottenham – and all in a couple of days, or just over.

Dr R. G. Miller
RAPWI RAMC

Why would a man, allegedly sane, strap a pack on his back, hook up to a static line, proceed to the open door of an aircraft in full flight and jump out? There must have been a streak of creative madness in each one of us. Such thoughts aside, why did we do it?

Looking back over all the years it is difficult to be quite sure. Lying deeply below the surface of conscious reflection there must have been two thoughts: a

'The volunteers gathered at Chaklala, near Rawalpindi. The aircraft used were the twenty-six seater twin-engined Dakotas.'

wholehearted commitment to the justice of the Allied cause and a feeling that one's rightful place lay at the scene of action. On the surface the thoughts were probably nearer to 'This sounds exciting. Let's go'.

The volunteers gathered at Chaklala near Rawalpindi. Most of those who came had never before been inside an aircraft. During the first week we did various exercises in the hangar, together with three familiarization aircraft flights. The second week was devoted to the seven training jumps. The aircraft used were the twenty-six seater twin-engined Dakotas. Three types of exercise were practised in the first week: jumping clear from the doorway of an aeroplane mock-up; wearing the parachute harness suspended by ropes from the roof of the hangar; and the more difficult landing drill. But most importantly we wore the cork helmet. To practise the landings we stood on a gallery alongside the hangar. Once we managed to transfer our weight to the rope attached to the roof, we swung out into the centre and landed on a mat floor.

The teams were trained in groups of ten men, each group with a sergeant instructor, whose patience, enthusiasm and encouragement created the right spirit for the team. Of course, the sergeant instructor jumped once with every team. Our instructor had made over a hundred and forty descents, and readily confessed that each time he jumped he still felt as though his heart was in his mouth. There was a parachute failure rate, officially given as 1 in 10,000. Such a disaster was awesome to watch and impossible to hide. Nevertheless, we were in the middle of a war and many men and women were facing risks far worse. Each person who jumped had a personal crisis to face, but few defaulted from the course. Without a certain degree of fatalism no one could have faced the awful side of war.

The first jump is an event which cannot be forgotten. The critical hooking-up to the static line which will pull the rigging lines and then the parachute from the pack, just before the parachutist falls away from the aircraft. The excitement, and then the strange quiet as the pilot throttles back the engines and puts the engine into a gentle dive, the red light over the door which turns to green – and away.

Two seconds' free-fall in a slipstream with a wind speed of more than 100 miles an hour is – to put it mildly – quite scary. The cross-ways rush of air is gradually replaced by an upwards thrust of air and two seconds is plenty long enough to be thoroughly frightened. But then, a pull on the shoulder straps, a pull which gradually becomes stronger and the rush of air dies away. You are suddenly left with a wonderful wide and peaceful scene as you float gently downwards.

But all too soon one must call to mind the landing drill and decide which particular roll would be appropriate. Done correctly, the bump on impact with the ground is not too bad. Then one unfastens the harness, collects the parachute, the team reassembles and one begins to wonder what all the fuss was about. The whole exercise is repeated on the following day, and in some respects the second jump seems more difficult than the first. After the second jump things become a little easier. Subsequent jumps are as a team known as 'sticks', where team spirit helps a great deal. One also develops the feeling that there is just a remote possibility that, supposing one's luck holds, the parachute might actually open. Then there are the specialized jumps, such as the night drop, or the kit bag drop – the latter involving having a kit bag attached to one leg. The kit bag was lowered on a rope until it dangled some 10 or 15 feet below and hits the ground first. After the seven descents we were awarded the coveted wings badge and given an increase in pay, a rise of a shilling a day which is the equivalent of £1.50 per month.

Following parachute training the units reassembled and re-formed on various sites in Central India where routine training continued. Further plans, of course, were much too secret for discussion. However, it seemed clear that after the capture of Rangoon the next major target would be the Malayan Peninsula.

Suddenly the unexpected happened: news broke of an atom bomb being dropped on Hiroshima in Japan. Would Japan surrender? The second atom bomb dropped on Nagasaki changed everything.

Within a few days, after a two-day holiday, a new plan was announced. Airborne teams were to be dropped into the various POW camps throughout the Far East. The code name RAPWI was introduced (Repatriation of Allied Prisoners of War and Internees). The teams were chosen and flown to Ceylon. We waited, then the announcement of the actual teams was made. I was fortunate to be included in the first team out, destined for Singapore, the Lion City of the East – the city of our dreams, the city captured three and a half years earlier by the Japanese. It was a city around which so many plans seemed to be centred, and here we were being asked to go under circumstances which would have been beyond the wildest flights of imagination less than a month earlier.

A short flight was made to the coast at China Bay, then we embarked on an adapted Liberator, modified for long-distance flights and for dropping parachutists. Did the Japanese know we were coming? Well, we've sent a signal. But was that really a good idea?

The drop was to be one week ahead of the planned seaborne landing in Singapore. Our instructions were firm. Until the seaborne landings the Japanese would be responsible for civil order, and in no way were we to seek or accept any position of command. And so the stage was set.

A heavily laden, four-engined piston-driven aircraft is not like a modern jet-propelled airliner, where the passengers are forced back into their seats by the acceleration as the plane takes off. The Liberator, especially when the loading margins were exceeded, literally fought its way into the air. Standing at the end of the runway with its brakes full on, one engine was revved up to maximum capacity and the plane shook, then the second, the third and fourth were run up. The sudden release of the brakes allowed maximum acceleration. Even so, the aircraft seemed to gather speed slowly and at midpoint of the runway was still gaining speed. The elements themselves seemed to be fighting for possession of the body and soul of the monster as the aircraft lifted off. The earth fell away from beneath the plane like a beautiful magic carpet and there was a sudden peace and quiet. We watched the coastline with its ocean breakers rolling in across the long stretch of sand, all in the evening light of sunset. It was quite unforgettable – as was the thought that tomorrow was another day.

During the ten-hour flight we wrote letters home to be taken back and posted by the aircrew. We ate a simple meal and had enough room to lie down and sleep with our parachute pack as a pillow. The long hours of darkness, the steady drone of the engines, the few lights seen from the flight deck and the occasional movement of a crew member – aside from these, our thoughts were our own. A

'I remember feeling, even in the wild rush of the slipstream, even before the parachute had opened, an immense relief that the critical moment now belonged to history . . .'

tiny group of people in the vast emptiness of the sky and over the sea, their watchful, wakeful eyes and thoughtful minds drawing ever nearer to their destination, almost 2,000 miles away. Daylight had arrived and the cabin crew were busy. A panel was removed from the base of the bomb bay. Through the opening we could see Singapore Island, separated from the mainland by the Straits of Jahore. A chute, like the kind often found in swimming pools, was fixed to a frame in the bomb bay. To exit the aircraft we would simply let go the sides of the chute.

I remember feeling, even in the wild rush of the slipstream, even before the parachute had opened, an immense relief that the critical moment now belonged to history, rather than being burdened with the uncertainty which quite unavoidably is always part of the future.

Once the parachute had opened there was a problem. The drop was on what is now Changi Airport but was then a bare military airstrip on the eastern tip of the island. Around the airstrip were a few single-storey, barrack-like buildings and I was drifting on to one of them. The flight harness of the parachute was connected to the canopy by four straps. In the theoretical part of our training we had been told that we could change the direction of our drift by pulling either on the left-hand or on the right-hand pair. However, there was little response to my efforts to correct my drift.

Remembering the drill – legs held lightly together, knees and hips slightly bent, arms firmly into the sides with elbows bent, spine and neck slightly flexed. I hit the ridge of the sloping roof and slithered down the rafters with an increasing clatter of tiles. Fortunately, the guttering came too; if it had resisted, the parachute would have emptied of air and the final fall could have been awkward. Everything landed in a heap on the ground. I got up, anatomically intact but minus the seat of my trousers and the heel of one boot.

Our six-man team consisted of two doctors, two medical orderlies and two signals officers. We collected ourselves, our bits and pieces and our belongings and assembled at an office at the end of the runway. We had been dropped in two 'sticks', each of three men, each stick being dropped on a separate run. Various supplies had also been dropped. We waved goodbye as the Liberator began its long journey back to Ceylon. Leaflets had been dropped on the previous day.

We met Japanese guards in the office and eventually a car arrived to drive us to Changi Jail. This was a massive grey-stoned edifice, erected just before the war as a civilian prison but used by the Japanese as a centre for their complex of POW camps. By the Japanese we were shown deference that could not be faulted. The servicemen who had formerly been POWs remarked on the complete and sudden change in the bearing and behaviour of the previously arrogant guards.

There were about ten or twelve military POW camps on the island, and one civilian internment camp at Sime Road. Shortages of everything had been severe and conditions were bleak and harsh. Nevertheless, a disciplined structure existed in each camp and medical officers were in post doing all they could under the very difficult circumstances. The incoming teams adopted an administrative role. We visited the different camps, heard of their needs and shortages, and through the signal officers we were able to arrange for further supplies in subsequent supply drops.

My visit to the Sime Road Camp was memorable. There was a wild enthusiasm in the inmates' cheering, an enthusiasm undoubtedly felt but not so uninhibitedly displayed in the military camps. Walking through cheering crowds was an experience, even if one lacked the heel of one boot and wore torn trousers.

Our team was quickly joined by another which had been dropped about two months earlier on to the mainland of Malaya to work with local underground units against the Japanese. When this team had heard the news of the Japanese surrender they formed a plan to be the first Allied troops to reach Singapore. They were not pleased to find our team had flown in from Ceylon. But the two

A Mosquito pilot of No. 221 Group saw written on the roof of Rangoon gaol the words 'JAPS GONE'. A Beaufighter of 177 Squadron took this photograph while on a recce flight.

teams quickly united in the common task of planning the evacuation from the camps and the distribution of supplies.

A week after our parachute drop the seaborne force sailed into Singapore harbour. Certain vessels were designated hospital ships to take home, via India, the sick and the wounded prisoners. The RAPWI teams were concerned with the organization of the transport and related arrangements between the camps and the hospital ships. There was a real sense of achievement as the first of these vessels left the dockside.

Captain Edward Hamlyn
RAPWI RAMC

Soon after the bombing of Hiroshima and Nagasaki, Jack Tomlinson and I were dropped on our own into a Japanese POW camp at Port Dickson in Malaya. We were supposed to prevent the Japanese guards killing their prisoners so as to destroy evidence of war crimes, and we were also supposed to succour the prisoners with food and medicines.

In the event, the containers dropped with us in the camp had been pilfered back at the home base. Not only had anything of any value been stolen but also the parachutes were missing. All our containers did a free-drop as a result. We had no food, no medical supplies, but a quantity of damaged and quite unusable automatic weapons.

Going into a potentially hostile environment wearing Red Cross arm bands and armed to the teeth was not a good idea. But fortunately the prisoners reached us before the Jap guards got to us and all the arms and ammunition which we had about our bodies vanished into thin air before the Japs caught a glimpse of them.

Jack and I turned out to be a major liability in the camp, for we were two extra mouths to feed and had brought no extra rations. So we decided to escape the camp. We were yellow with mepacrine, as well nourished as only a Jap could be in that situation, and left camp in the commandant's car. I was wearing his hat, Jack lay on the floor, and all before the commandant was up and about in the morning.

We later managed to open a hospital in the interior and ran into trouble persuading the natives to come for treatment. To get into an army truck with someone wearing uniform was firmly fixed in their minds as being the start of a journey to hell, with torture and certain death at the end of it. So until they learned to trust us and came to associate these two boisterous and very unusual 'Japanese soldiers' with a degree of kindness and good care, we had to force them aboard at gun-point. Loosing off a few rounds soon convinced the villagers that our guns were loaded.

We heard on the grapevine that Red Cross supplies had arrived at Singapore. This was some 250 miles away and the only hope of getting any of these goodies was to make the journey in person. Arriving in Singapore with no authority whatever for my existence, and my uniform having long since been rendered completely unrecognizable, my official application for Red Cross supplies drew a complete blank. With no time to spare we drove to the docks and started loading, only to be arrested by the military police and hauled back in front of the bureaucrats. I told Jack to continue loading and to be ready for a quick getaway.

Back at the offices, I excused myself to go to the lavatory, climbed out of the window and down a fire escape. Walking brisk and confident up to the self-same military policeman and his jeep I demanded an immediate return to the docks. 'Yes, Sir!' he said. And thus it came about that with a full load of Red Cross supplies I was driven flat out back to my hospital at Bahau before dark. And that was the carefree, happy-go-lucky manner in which Jack and I brought the death rate in our bit of Malaya down to zero.

From   *Forward Base, Psychological Warfare Division, SEAC.*

Translation Japanese Leaflet No SJ/141

JAPAN SURRENDERS UNCONDITIONALLY

The Japanese forces have surrendered unconditionally and the war is over.

Allied aircraft are dropping leaflets in English, Dutch or Urdu giving instructions to Allied prisoners of war to remain quietly where they are.

Japanese guards must see that the prisoners get those leaflets and see that the prisoners are treated with every attention. The guards should then withdraw to their own quarters.

All Japanese officers and soldiers will be held personally responsible for the good treatment, care and proper feeding of all prisoners of war and internees.

Translation leaflet No. SJ/141, showing the English version of the leaflets dropped.

W. Adams
357 SQUADRON RAF

In early 1945 I was on supply dropping operations with 357 Squadron flying Dakotas from a temporary airfield in Burma. The squadron had been formed at Digri the year before for special duties in south-east Asia. Supply drops to guerilla forces in Burma were made from Bengal using Hudson aircraft.

By January 1945 Dakotas had taken over from the Hudsons and Lysanders, the latter operating landings and pick-ups from isolated airstrips in enemy-held territory. Some of our trips were five or six hours in duration and we didn't always find the dropping zone so it meant bringing the supplies back again.

We often experienced hair-raising incidents. Being the wireless operator I used to sit in the second pilot's seat during take off and landing so as to operate the flaps and undercarriage; also to push my hand up behind the throttle levers as the pilot moved them forward. There was the occasion when we were taking off with a full load of parachute packages. We were two thirds of the way down the runway when I noticed the speed indicator reading zero. I shot a quick glance at the pilot who immediately opened up the throttles wider and took the Dakota almost to the end of the runway. He gave me the 'up undercarriage' sign, pulled back on the control column and, thankfully, we rose into the air.

On 18 July we made an emergency landing at Chittagong with engine trouble. Repairs were not completed until the following day. Despite not having any mosquito nets we slept in the aircraft overnight. After a restless night beneath a hastily rigged camouflage net I counted only twenty-four mosquito bites next morning.

On our way back to Rangoon after one particularly long and arduous trip, we became aware of a fuel shortage. As we circled the airfield at Mingaladon we saw rows of white uniformed troops lining the runway, with a brass band and gold-braided figures on the concourse.

Calling up for permission to land, the pilot was told to hold off as they were expecting Lord Louis Mountbatten's plane any minute. Explaining the desperate fuel

The SPE/1 leaflet scattered over the POW camps in Burma and Siam by 357 Squadron Dakotas on 22 August 1945.

situation we were allowed to land, go to the end of the runway, and quietly disappear. As we came in to land I was thinking, 'Now I know how a mongrel would feel at Crufts', and also wondered what the reception committee were thinking seeing an ordinary old green Dakota arriving instead of a shining white one.

We had by now done some intensive flying, going to such places as Calcutta, Rangoon, Singapore, China Bay, Bangkok, Kuala Lumpur, Penang and Saigon, and some not-so-well-known places in between. At Rangoon our job was the evacuation of POWs. First they had to be assembled at a suitable pick-up point. In the meantime, however, we flew over the POW camps dropping food and supplies, also leaflets in English and Japanese, telling the inmates and their guards what to do and what not to do. After the official drops we would do a low-level run throwing out bundles of newspapers and magazines. We flew so low on one occasion I am sure a chap almost took a bundle out of my hands.

When picking up the POWs almost every day we visited such places as Phit Buri, Takli, Prama and Tavoy, and brought out the first civilian internees.

I never was one of those keen on flying for flying's sake, but I always felt comfortable and at ease in the Dakota, more so, I think, than I would have done in any other aircraft. Of course, I was extremely fortunate in being teamed up with a first-class pilot and navigator, which made a world of difference.

'As we circled the Mingaladon airfield we saw rows of white uniformed troops lining the runway . . .' Lord Louis Mountbatten, Supreme Commander SEAC, arrives at Chittagong in his white Dakota.

'. . . we flew over the POW camps dropping food and supplies, also leaflets in English and Japanese.' One of the leaflets printed in Japanese.

Tom McKie
SCOTS GREYS POW

I had left the Forestry Commission in Scotland before the war to join the Scots Greys; fought in France and Belgium – survived Dunkirk, then sent as escort to the German and Italian internees on the SS *Andora Star*. She was torpedoed just 14 hours out of Liverpool en route to Canada.

After that ordeal I was posted to the Lanarkshire Yeomanry with 155 Field Regiment. RA, and sent to India for a couple of months, then travelled to Malaya in open cattle trucks to join the 11th Indian Div. After a foray into what was then Siam (Thailand), blowing up ammunition dumps, we had to fight our way through the jungle back to Singapore where, after a fortnight of bloodshed, British troops eventually surrendered to the Japanese.

My regiment was the first to be slung into Changi Jail. We were three to a tiny cell whose only facility was a concrete bench, used as a bed. We heard we were being punished for damage we had inflicted upon the Japanese Imperial Army.

Our first work was heartbreaking. We'd march to the docks to clear the corpses of Chinese from the barbed wire entanglements. The Japs had taken them out to sea, then machine gunned them. We cleared up their remains as they were washed ashore. The heat and stench of rotting flesh will never leave me. The flies, clustered like grapes.

We bent double as 15 stone of cement in three bags, was slung across our shoulders, bleeding after hours of toil in the soupy climate. We dared not take a breather. If we had stopped running up the gang-plank to load the Japanese ships berthed at Singapore docks, the guards would have beaten us unconscious. I saw it happen all too often, for once on the ground, we would lie there until work had finished. Then – and only then, would we be allowed to carry the fallen back to camp. We gritted our teeth and began running, stick-like legs gathering strength from GOD knows where.

I hate them still. I hated them for their cruelty when I was their prisoner and nothing has happened to change my mind. When you have seen good lads beaten, left in the blistering sun for hours, then slipping towards death because they have no strength left to go on living, you learn to hate your captors fast.

Sometime later, fed just one beakerful of cooked rice daily, we were moved to the ruins of the Great World amusement park and established a precarious means of survival. Working on the docks meant we could steal to survive. There were warehouses, which were full of tinned stuff waiting to be shipped to Japan. We filched as much as we could, sold it to the Chinese and, with the cash they paid us, bought food.

Occasionally the native Chinese would take pity on us skeletal men and slip us loaves and dried fish. Those of us who became ill were tended by British military doctors and nurses. When loading rice, we used to break open sacks and fill our pockets with it – also tinned pineapple, a vital food source because the Japs provided only a starvation diet on which men would die.

We discovered tons of medical supplies and were able to make false bottoms to the trucks – knowing they would end up with medical staff at Changi Jail. Our greatest coup was finding rows of British lorries seized by the Japanese, and destined to be shipped back for use by the Jap Army. We drained the engine oil and replaced it with battery acid, aware that the engines would burn out quickly.

For the next two years, our dwindling band of comrades were slave-labour on the 'Death Railway' between Siam and Burma. I can recall, in sharp focus, the late night burial-parties for the emaciated British corpses, the task of holding hands with our mates through the dark night – knowing they would die before dawn. We dug a moat for our own graves at Nacom Paton but, before our bodies could fill it, we were marched to the coast to embark for the journey to Japan. We were sunk by an American submarine. The Jap Navy picked us up and dumped us on the quayside at Pat Pong, where we lived like vagrants.

I was a prisoner in 17 different camps, weighed five stone and felt my body weakening as every day passed. About one thousand of us went into the last

'I can recall, in sharp focus, the late night burial-parties . . . the task of holding hands with our mates through the dark night – knowing they would die before dawn.'

camp and only 200 remained when the Jap guards, realising they had lost the war, suddenly – and without warning, disappeared. We were alone in the jungle then. No body knew we were there, just 200 of us and only a few fit to walk.

We eventually set off in different directions, agreeing to stagger back and report on what we had found. I struck lucky. It took me two-and-a-half days to struggle across the Burmese hills to reach a Siamese air-strip, where contact was made with the British and my mates were brought in.

But fate had one final kick in the teeth for these men. Two of the four Dakotas taking us out, flew into an electric storm as we headed for Rangoon and freedom. They crashed into hills – killing every one on board.

We – the lucky ones, were almost force-fed for a fortnight before embarking for Liverpool in a troopship. The scars on the back of my hands are a reminder of where – all too frequently, the Japanese guards used to stub out their cigarettes. They were the cruellest people I have ever had the misfortune to meet. Just don't try and tell me they have changed, eh?

Kay Smith
VAD

Our patients were recently liberated POWs being taken by train to British military hospitals. It was a sad job. The majority looked like very old men, none weighed over 5 stone and the smell was awful. All of them had the most terrible ulcers and running sores, which had been treated by wrapping them in filthy germ-infested oily rags. Some had badly scarred backs due to beatings, one especially had had all his teeth kicked out. The tales of atrocities they told us were so shocking I tried in vain not to listen. One young lad, for that was all he was, had a makeshift plaster cast on his leg and was being driven mad by the irritation. The medical officer quickly cut off the cast. Under it the leg was a mass of writhing maggots! Two of us tried to remove them with our combs but in the end we had to pull each one off with eyebrow tweezers. Wrapping the maggots in paper we quickly threw them out of the window.

Our next meal included rice. The grains looked so similar to the maggots we just could not eat anything. There was no water on the train and the men were so parched that when we stopped at the next station I bartered away my nurse's fob watch for some oranges to ease their thirst.

M.W. Swinhoe-Phelan
ROYAL ENGINEERS

We arrived at Bombay to the distinctive odour of India, then we were off to Calcutta to fight our way through pedestrians, cows, rickshaws, handcarts, pony-

'. . . I joined 6th Battalion Royal Engineers on the Sittang River, where I was given a company of 120 of our men plus 200 Japanese Surrendered Personnel (JSPs).' JSPs loading a Dakota.

pulled tongas, cyclists and maniac taxi-drivers. There was the normal army cock-up and although we should have had priority travel, it was four days before we sailed for Rangoon. After four more days we approached Burma and were dazzled by the gleaming golden spire of the Shwe Dagong pagoda shining in the morning sunlight.

In September I joined 6th Battalion Royal Engineers on the Sittang River where I was put in charge of a company of 120 of our men plus 200 Japanese Surrendered Personnel (JSPs). Their own officer was fairly presentable but his men seemed in very poor shape, with sores and blood-stained bandages covering most of their frail bodies. They were in need of a proper meal as they had been existing on a handful of rice daily and not much else so they lacked stamina. Still, supervised by my VCOs and NCOs they worked with gusto. We had a 10 mile stretch of road to repair. Down this each day a small truck would drive slowly issuing commands by loudspeakers for unsurrendered Japanese to obey their Emperor's orders to come out of the jungle and lay down their weapons. However onerous the job, it went like clockwork with everything being done at the double. Even huge baulks of timber and 1 cwt bags of cement were carried on the run. And they never had cause to complain and neither did I.

CHAPTER SIX

'We Emptied our Bladders . . .'

When, in August 1943, Admiral Lord Louis Mountbatten was instructed at the Quebec Conference to create an inter-service, inter-Allied command, to be known as South East Asia Command (SEAC), he made notes of the most urgent points to be dealt with. Among them was the need for an inter-service daily newspaper. He felt strongly that to fight a successful campaign of indefinite duration, thousands of miles away from home, everyone involved needed to feel they were in touch with the latest news. He conceived the paper as one of the psychological foundations of the new command, a project that would help to express his policy of keeping the men informed of what was happening at home as well as on the fighting fronts.

Lord Louis recognized the importance of having an impartial newspaper, edited as fairly as was possible, but as there was a limit to the supply of newsprint, it was kept to just four pages.

When the paper was launched on 10 January 1944, General Slim was commanding a force then charged with keeping the Japanese out of India. That force was already the biggest of the British Imperial armies but its name, the 14th Army, was still on the secret list. There was already a feeling among the men that there, on the borders of Burma, they were unheeded, unsung, forgotten by the people back home.

Mountbatten had decided to enlist Frank Owen as his first editor. In at the birth of the SEAC newspaper were many names synonymous with the art of journalism – Ian Coster, Len Jackson, Tom Wilcox, Harry Stainforth, Reg Foster, Vince Tillotson, Bill Duff and George Chisholm. They were all painstaking in their approach to reporting – they had to be, with a seven-day-a-week job involving night work.

It was the first inter-services newspaper in any army command, anywhere, and from the beginning its staff was drawn from all three services. Its readers too represented all three services stationed in India, Burma and, later, all points east.

This was the first SEAC all services newspaper in any command, anywhere, and from the beginning its staff was drawn from all three services.

From the word go the newspaper was a triumph. Americans provided the photographs and transport in the early stages. All British services joined in production and distribution, the RAF providing the aircraft to fly the regular daily run to focal points on the front. From there army transport carried it to forward units and some even turned up in the most remote and isolated areas. The RAF squadrons on low-level bombing and strafing missions would often divert off course to drop a bundle to some jungle outpost. They took them to General Messervy's 7th Indian Division when they were cut off in February 1944, and dropped them to the besieged Imphal and Kohima during the battles that have since been recognized as the turning point in the whole campaign. At almost every major development of the campaign, a SEAC man went up to the front to cover the story.

When the days of the struggle were over and after the atom bombs had so dramatically changed the situation, the separation of SEAC from India loomed, and the newspaper ceased production in Calcutta and moved to Singapore.

This is the last SEAC newspaper, No. 852, published for the last time in Singapore on 15 May 1946.

Through two and a half years, without interruption, the journalists had enjoyed the greatest privilege of freedom they were ever likely to experience: the freedom to give the news with no consideration of 'policy'. It had been a unique experience, where proprietorial interest and prejudice were dirty words and where freedom to express their own views – right or wrong – was encouraged.

The last SEAC newspaper, No. 852, was published at 127 Cecil Street, Singapore, by the Straits Times; it rolled off the printing machines on Wednesday 15 May 1946, its editor then was Tom Wilcox.

George Paxton
680 FLOTILLA ROYAL MARINE

After my initial training at Lympstone in 1943, I became a Royal Marine signalman, but when the course was over it was soon realized there were too many of us so fifty were retrained to work as stoker/drivers on landing craft.

Having learned the art of ship-to-shore communication using Aldis lamp, flags, Morse code (visual and wireless) and even heliograph, we were soon involved with internal combustion engines, the construction of all types of ship and craft, and practical seamanship in handling small vessels, particularly landing craft.

In June 1944 we were climbing the gangway of the P & O steamship SS *Maloja* at Greenock, destination unknown. Eventually we sailed through the Red Sea, the Gulf of Aden and then into the Indian Ocean. Because of the intense heat we were allowed to sleep on the upper deck which was a vast improvement from being packed like sardines below in a stifling C deck. We arrived in the monsoon period and the heavens opened up with a fierce intensity. The SS *Maloja* looked like a mobile Chinese laundry with every inch of deck space completely covered with drenched hammocks and clothing.

At Bombay one morning on parade our CO produced a piece of foolscap upon which was typed all our names. He told us we would be split into two groups. He then tore the page in half, giving one half to each lieutenant standing on either side of him, and said, 'This half to Burma, this half to South India'. By this democratic means I was allocated to South India. The Burma half of the group went to places like Akyab and Cheduba in the Arakan, ferrying Gurkhas up and down the chaungs. My group ferried urgent supplies and personnel to and from naval vessels in the Palk Strait between India and Ceylon.

Our craft were American-built landing craft made of plywood but with an armoured ramp door and propelled by a Grey Marine six-cylinder diesel engine. The ferrying was mostly done between liberty ships, but on numerous occasions we served HMS *Sheffield* of the Royal Navy and HMAS *Sydney* of the Australian Navy.

We were in a Bombay cinema when a hand-written message suddenly appeared on the screen to say hostilities had ceased. Another message followed ordering all British personnel back to their respective camps. We left – jildi! Although the war was over the fighting was not, and we soon found ourselves in landing craft either slung from davits or lashed to the deck of the British crewed liberty ship MV *Empire Victory*, bound for Port Dickson, Malaya, to round up pirates and bandits. Also on board were the Pioneer Corps and Royal Engineers. On arrival the landing craft were lowered over the side and we fixed up our identification sign – D96 – above the wheelhouse. We were now part of 'W' Force, two flotillas, Nos 680 and 681.

We must have been the second wave after the assault troops had landed the previous day. The Royal Marine officer who climbed the rickety wooden ladder on the jetty was heard to say afterwards, 'I was very apprehensive about sticking my head above the jetty in case it was lopped off. Much to my relief and surprise, the whole Japanese garrison was lined up behind their CO, who stepped forward, saluted, then handed me his sword as a token of surrender'.

We ferried army personnel, 15 cwt trucks, generators, rations (some marked with a crescent for Indian Muslim troops), stretchers and tents and just about everything you could think of. Soon afterwards the *Empire Victory* weighed anchor and we were directed to the Royal Navy Fleet Auxiliary oil tanker *Ennerdale*. We quickly made use of her showers and toilet facilities for a couple of days, but for dhobying we towed our soiled clothing on a line astern of our landing craft, losing a few items in the process.

The sudden capitulation meant the Japanese authorities in the area continued to be active for a couple of weeks, until an Allied civil authority could be organized. Even the Japanese newspapers continued publication announcing the demise of Japanese banks and businesses. It was during this period that worthless currency notes were being shovelled out of the back of lorries like confetti.

We set up our tents on the beach and got to know the local people. Our Craven A cigarettes were bartered for fresh produce and I recall that our tinned herrings in tomato sauce were in great demand by the Malays, Sikhs and Portuguese Eurasians.

'For some reason he also forgot to switch on the bilge exhaust fans before pressing the start button. There was the inevitable explosion . . .' The funeral of Marine B. Mellor.

Soon after the British resumed control, reports came in that a few subversive elements were causing trouble in the rubber plantations. There was one particular moonless night that I will never forget. We had been rushed out to subdue an anticipated raid. It was pitch black and we were patrolling some buildings when I decided to check up on my mate. He was missing. I looked everywhere. On the edge of a thick jungle in the dead of night it was quite eerie on your own. I thought the bandits had spirited my mate away but, in reality, it was just a call of nature.

A couple of weeks later we took a platoon of Gurkhas to an island just north of Penang, where pirates were said to be molesting local fishing boats. We managed to apprehend one or two suspicious craft. I hated being shut away in the unbearable heat of the engine-room, but the rumour that pirates sometimes lobbed grenades down the ventilator shafts of inquisitive vessels did not help either.

I recall only one fatality. The accident occurred one morning when my pal Ben Mellor went on board his landing craft to carry out the usual checks before starting engines. He had done those morning checks a thousand times and yet this time he forgot to open the hatches. There would have been a build-up of fumes from the fuel tanks in the bilges overnight. For some reason he also forgot to switch on the bilge exhaust fans before pressing the starter button. There was the inevitable explosion which could be heard miles away. Ben died of terrible burns within the day.

It was the first week in April 1946, when we boarded a 6,000 tonne LST at Singapore bound for England. We eventually arrived at Chatham, entrained for London and were soon demobbed. How green the fields looked from the carriage windows.

C. Tilley
PATHFINDERS INDIAN AIRBORNE

As the Pathfinders was an independent company, things had become rather lax, and the coming of the end of the war meant a tightening up for us. Ginger Doughty the Provost Sergeant was waiting to go home at any time, so Levy was given a couple of stripes and put on the staff. The very next morning, as soon as reveille had blown, Corporal Levy was round as quick as lightning getting everyone out of bed. For the next week Levy was everywhere. Do this, do that and do the other.

So we decided to do something about it. One night at lights out Levy was around. 'Get that light out! Get that light out!' The whole camp went quiet. Everyone waited in expectation. Then we heard a shriek. Levy had got into bed and as his foot reached the bottom he thought it came into contact with a snake.

There was bedlam for a few minutes. Levy jumped out of bed, got tangled up with the mossey net and fell over in his haste. He shouted, 'I've been bitten by a snake!' By this time everyone was up and wanting to kill the snake for him. I still cannot remember who put that bull frog in his bed.

I used to do a bit of painting during my off-duty time, and it soon became so that the lads would ask me to paint their photo albums. I was asked to paint the Pathfinder crest on the sergeants' mess wall for Christmas. Paint was always scarce in those days, so after scrounging around I managed to improvise with mepacrine tablets for yellow, Reckitt's Blue, chicken blood for red and brown and charcoal from the char-wallah's brazier for black.

At the beginning I used to paint at night after duty and was paid with whatever I could drink. Everyone liked the finished artwork and suggested I should brighten up the walls with something else. I had just been given a portfolio of pin-ups by the artist David Wright, and they asked me to paint them on the walls life-size. After the first was completed I was allowed to miss

'Paint was always scarce in those days, so after scrounging around I managed to improvise with mepacrine tablets for yellow, Reckitts Blue, chicken blood for red and brown, and charcoal from the char-wallah's brazier for black.'

'I had just been given a portfolio of
pin-ups by the artist David Wright,
and they asked me to paint them on
the walls life-size.'

duties and get on with the job. Then the officers' mess decided they should have
their walls similarly decorated. The CO wanted one done on a board so that he
could take it with him wherever he went!

During a party one night Major Archie Wavell MC, of the 2nd Battalion
Black Watch (Lord Wavell's son), saw my work and asked if I would paint views
of Scotland (not pin-ups), for his education centre. I continued painting until
the Pathfinders were disbanded. Lord knows how much I drank in those days!

Ken Day
BLACK WATCH NEWSLETTER

Off to the pictures – in the jungle. It is 1900 hrs and the sun, edging towards
the horizon, is leaving a trail of colour – glory in the fast darkening sky. It is
very necessary that the sun should set, for the show can't begin until darkness
envelops this little jungle clearing in India.

You see, our cinema lacks a roof. Its four walls are brick up to a height of three feet and bamboo up to where the roof isn't. At a gap in one wall, we pay to go in. Those who can still sit in plush seats at the local Odeon at home would gladly pay to get out! We buy 'front stalls' – a dozen rows of backless wooden benches – and mind the nails. The 'chocolate girl' is a moustached black-skinned fruit-wallah who takes our rupee notes. Soon the floor is littered with monkey-nut shells and orange peel, while late-comers are liable to add to the interest of the evening by slipping on a carpet of banana skins.

The sun has now set. Inside it is standing room only. The time is 1940 hrs – ten minutes after starting time. But we are used to these delays. Any one of three things might not have turned up: (a) the Manager; (b) the projectionist; (c) the film. The original gramophone that Edison invented is whirling round records that have seen, not their best days, so much as their best years. The front stalls are bawling for the show to begin, while half-dreading that it will. The film billed for tonight is *Lovers All*, starring Flo Vaseur and Maurice Madness. Never heard of them? Probably not. They came to the screen about the time the magic lantern went out. The younger soldiers among us were dribbling in their perambulators when *Lovers All* was released.

At last! Someone mercifully stops the gramophone. The curtains part to reveal the seductive Flo on the dirty bed-linen. Now don't get me wrong! It isn't that sort of picture. The dirty bed-linen is just our name for the screen. Within ten minutes the film has broken down. We wait in the darkness, eyeing the sky overhead and speculating on the chances of a reminder from the monsoon.

The gramophone starts again. It stops, and Flo Vaseur reappears – but not where she left off. Oh, no. It is now a different scene entirely. Maurice Madness, who was a thousand miles away at the point where the film broke down, is now with her in her boudoir. Any one of three reasons might be advanced for this technical hitch: (a) it is what is known as a clumsy cut; (b) a lump of film fell out of the train on the way up; (c) the projectionist has been drinking toddy again.

We are used to these things. We are tolerant. Maurice has taken Flo in his arms. 'My own!' he husks, or rather the prehistoric speakers husk for him. 'Darling!' she croaks, and brings down the house. 'Get cracking, Maurice!' comes from the four anna benches. 'Take her, she's yours for the picking', comes from the nine annas. This and much unprintable advice is yelled gleefully. But before Maurice can get cracking the apparatus beats him to it. The film has broken down again. Another delay, during which banana skins are thrown at the screen.

Flo Vaseur reappears on the screen as the first drops of rain descend on the audience. Monsoon capes are hurriedly put on. Maurice Madness continues to husk and croak. But the interest of the audience has been switched to the skies. It is now raining in torrents. Stepping over puddles and skirting clumps of orange peel the patrons are making for the exit. We are picking our way down the pathway formed by the bare feet of a million peasants – back to the camp near the village.

MONSOON

Eck dum, eck dum, the monsoon's come
The basha walls are drawn,
When strong men mutter, grim and glum,
'We'll all be drowned by dawn.'

They decko through the water spout,
Observing with a grin
The flying dhobi, flying out,
To fetch his washing in!

The fruit wallah has jildi jowd
Complete with nuts and mangoes,
The char-wallah was heard to mutter,
'You've had your egg banjos.'

The QM sorting suits,
Gave a loud and horrible sigh
As several pairs of army boots,
Float by before his eyes.

It is time to hit the charpoy,
And get below your net.
The flying ants will soon be here
And other things, I bet.

Eck dum, eck dum, the monsoon's come
No use to sigh and sob!
Just fill the mugs with char, old pal,
And talk about demob.

                                        Anon

Major John Shave
411 PARA SQUADRON

I was in charge of 411 Para Squadron at Malir near Karachi. It consisted of three troops, two of them Mahrattas and the other Punjabi Mussulmans. We always called them 'jawans' (meaning soldiers) and never sepoys, which I think was a term restricted to infantrymen. The Punjabi Mussulmans had been with the parachute brigade dropped to recapture Rangoon. Incidentally, they are now part of the Indian Army.

We dropped in what was probably the last demonstration jump before Independence. I had been giving the squadron some intensive training which may have been why we were selected. Final take off was from Bhopal in Dakotas (my pilot was Flight Lieutenant Burberry of the mackintosh firm), and the DZ (dropping zone) was the maidan at Mhow. The jawans went in fine style and landed complete in three sticks. Unfortunately, the explosives and other engineer gear fell across some barrack blocks and that rather spoilt it. The demonstration for the School of Infantry was not a complete success. But that is the nature of almost all airborne operations.

'The jawans went in fine style and landed complete in three sticks. Unfortunately, the explosives and other engineer gear fell across some barrack blocks and that rather spoilt it.'

Andy Dickson
ROYAL SIGNALS

This recital of wasted journeys across the sub-continent sums up the muddles and inefficiencies of the time. With such monumental cock-ups it is surprising the British helped win a war at all!

The war was coming to a close when I joined the Royal Signals to become a telephone operator. It was over by the time I set sail on the converted Dutch troopship *Subajak*, to reach Bombay in November 1945. The usual trooptrain scenario only existed to get the BORs from one place to another in the least possible comfort.

First we went to Kalyan; thence to the signals depot at Mhow; next a draft of 110 men went to South East Asia Command in two separate parties, ours going to a transit camp in Madras. The other party went to a different camp. Thanks to a slip-up we stayed in Madras for three whole weeks while a second party went to Kandy in Ceylon.

Eventually the first party, myself included, arrived at Kandy only to find that SEAC had already moved to Singapore! So back we went to Madras for another three weeks. From there we were sent to Badadi, an ex-Italian POW camp just west of Bangalore where we stayed for a fortnight. By now we were experts on travelling in India. So it was really no problem when we got sent back to Madras – except that we entrained for Calcutta en route to Barrackpore. Surprisingly, we were then stuck there until May 1946.

How I arrived back at Madras I will never know – perhaps it was something to do with travel sickness, a new form which attacked the mind. Within a month I was being sent to GHQ in New Delhi where our billets were near the Indian parliamentary buildings. We remained there until August, when the states of India and Pakistan were formed. We actually used telephones there in the exchange when Muslims were leaving for Pakistan. Occasionally we were used as armed escort for Muslims going to Pakistan by train across the new boundary lines near Lahore. Finally, on 26 February 1948, we left Karachi with the 2nd Battalion Black Watch, virtually the last of the British Army to leave Pakistan.

Ron Wintle
INDIAN AIRBORNE

For me VJ-Day in Bilaspur was a bit of an anticlimax. I had dysentery and was in a bad way. The monsoon was at its height and there was a small ration of beer – not that I was in any condition to drink it. Instead the lads, rather unsteadily, carried me on a stretcher to the medical tent through torrential rain and thick mud, while thunderflashes exploded all around us thrown by men celebrating.

'Our battery was chosen to represent Indian Airborne in the Victory Parade at New Delhi. Taking the salute were the Viceroy Lord Wavell and General Auchinleck . . .'

'During the parade, however, students in Connaught Square threw bags of flour everywhere.'

In Bilaspur – surely the most horrible place in India – there was a sudden outbreak of ringworm, so severe that the battery was divided into Ringworm Groups and Non-ringworm Groups to try and prevent further infestation. Ringworm usually affected the most sensitive areas of one's body. The treatment applied was Whitfields Ointment, a substance which stung viciously. There was a slow march to the medical tent then a quick march to the showers afterwards.

Our battery was chosen to represent Indian Airborne in the Victory Parade at New Delhi. It was a long journey across the Sind Desert to Lahore, most of it over narrow roads made up of brick, sand and dirt, and it was essential to keep one set of wheels on the brick sections. Taking the salute were the Viceroy Lord Wavell and General Auchinleck, while overhead there was an RAF fly-past. Altogether it was quite spectacular.

During the parade, however, students in Connaught Square threw bags of flour everywhere. But through it all the Gurkha Rifles' band was magnificent, playing with imperturbable precision.

P. Chapman
2ND BATTALION BLACK WATCH

The main battalion party left Bilaspur for Karachi in the middle of January 1946, the five-day journey being broken at Delhi for several hours, when most of the party were given a meal at the Wavell Canteen. During the halt, the pipe band played a selection, much appreciated by the large crowd which soon gathered on the platform. In addition, Archie Wavell (son of the Viceroy and former company commander of the 2nd Black Watch), Nigel Noble and Bill Bryce visited us at the station. Perhaps the outstanding feature of the journey was the never-failing supply of char at every halt, no matter how short.

On arrival at Karachi the battalion was placed in temporary quarters for three weeks, after which we moved to Malir Camp. It was a large camp, taken over from the US Army. The companies were in barrack rooms, fitted with electric lights and – joy of joys – electric fans. The battalion area was blessed with a swimming pool, tennis courts and a couple of football pitches. The latter were cursed with acres of sand, soft and several inches thick, guaranteed to break the hearts of all cooks and conscientious shoe-shiners.

On 21 February, mutiny broke out on board the RIN sloop, HMIS *Hindustan*. The battalion was called out in the middle of the afternoon, and by dusk was standing by in Napier Barracks, Karachi. Several ratings from shore establishments on Manora Island had boarded and taken over the sloop. They had refused to leave and began firing on anyone who tried to board the ship. At midnight, the battalion was ordered to proceed to Manora, as trouble was expected from the shore establishments, HMIS *Bahadur, Chamak* and *Himalaya*, and from the naval AA school on the island. We were ferried across in launches and landing craft. D Company was the first across, and they immediately proceeded to the northern end of the island to the *Chamak*. The remainder of the battalion stayed at the southern end of the island. Next morning the astonished residents woke up to find the Black Watch all over the island. No one knew we had landed at night.

The first incident to happen that morning was the surrender of the ratings on the *Hindustan*, after half an hour's action during which they fired their 4 in guns blindly at Karachi. British guns replied with more accuracy at point-blank range and a white flag was soon hoisted through a hatch. But that appeared to be a signal for trouble to break out on the *Bahadur*. Several officers were thrown out by the ratings and the situation became serious. Soon after midday the battalion was ordered to take over *Bahadur*, and then the other establishments on the island. By the evening D Company was in possession of the AA school and *Chamak*, B Company had taken the *Himalaya*, while the rest of the battalion were in *Bahadur*. The mutiny was over.

The Black Watch remained on the island for several days, just in case of further trouble. A Company was detached to act as reserve during the civil disturbances which followed the mutiny. The disturbances over, the rest of the battalion's stay on Manora included swimming, fishing and mounting guard. The favourite guard was on board the *Hindustan*, despite the damage sustained by the ship. It is rather typical of the Jocks that, after two days, they were playing their 1st XI at football, beating the *Bahadur* team 3–1.

Revd John Marshall
ROYAL ARTILLERY

I was ordered to take my troop to the docks on the Thursday, one troop, R Battery, being already there in support of the infantry. It was my own C Troop, however, which was asked to do the dirty work. I decided to have one gun forward, partly shielded by a dockyard building and heavily sandbagged. The other three guns of the troop would be out of sight and firing indirectly.

I was not at all pleased to be told by the brigadier in charge of the whole operation to use the clock tower as my observation post, simply because it stuck out like a sore thumb. The ultimatum to the mutineers was due to expire at 10.30 a.m. next morning but my fears seemed well-founded when some ratings on board the *Hindustan* trained the aft-gun at me in my OP.

The account in the *Statesman* is not accurate in detail. I kept a diary in those days and it is open before me as I write now, nearly fifty years later. The expiry time had long passed and there was no message from the ship or any movement. So we gave them three minutes' grace before opening fire at 10.33 a.m. My sergeant's first shot was on target, he firing over open sights and directly. I directed ranging shots with the other three guns and scored a hit with the second.

Meanwhile, on board the *Hindustan* they began to open fire and several shells whizzed past my OP – fortunately without hitting it. Later we discovered the shells had failed to explode when they fell in Karachi itself. They had not been primed! It was not long before the mutineers cleared the decks and took cover. My one gun firing directly was so effective that I ordered the others to cease firing. My decision proved correct because at 10.51 a.m. a white flag suddenly appeared through a hatchway of the *Hindustan*. They had already stopped firing. British naval personnel removed the casualties and then the remainder of the crew.

Afterwards I visited the ship. It was not a pretty sight, of course, although I did take a certain amount of pride in the excellent shooting of my troop. But I had an overwhelming feeling of great sadness. These young Indian ratings, many of them still in their teens, had paid a heavy price for allowing themselves to be misguided into mutiny. The ship's superstructure was an absolute mess, for we had aimed above sea level. I imagine it was repairable. Sadly, much of the human damage could not be repaired.

'My one gun firing directly was so effective that I ordered the others to cease firing . . . at 10.51 a.m. a white flag suddenly appeared through a hatchway of the *Hindustan*.'

Lieutenant Colonel C.D.C. Frith OBE
SOMERSET LIGHT INFANTRY

I arrived in early 1945 and was billeted at the Taj Hotel, Bombay, not then the luxurious place it has since become. It was no more than a transit camp for officers with four to a room, no air-conditioning of course. But after the rigid austerity of Britain the shops were very smart and well-stocked. I was able to send home some good rugs and a beautifully decorated porcelain tea-set (made in England), a complete contrast to the plain crockery allowed at home.

Bombay was full of beggars, and one wondered if the many children to be seen on the streets had been deliberately maimed so as to increase the sympathy of prospective donors. There was the constant whine of 'Baksheesh, sahib'. The young boys pursued us, attempting to beguile us with cries of, 'You want nice "bibi", sahib? My sister she very nice – very clean'. The less salubrious parts of the city stank of open sewers, with Indians carrying out bodily functions in the open. The villages, though, were cleaner but smelled only of livestock, food and cooking fires. The fires were fuelled by dried cow pats. Women could be seen squatting in groups, slapping the dung from one hand to the other, fashioning it into round shapes before drying the pats in the hot sun. Surprisingly, it made an aromatic fuel, but one always wondered whether those same hands that shaped the fuel pats also made the very similar-sized chapattis.

Our pioneer sergeant and I were deputed to get rid of a tiger causing some concern in a jungle near our camp at Saugor. The villagers rigged up a charpoy in a tree with a young goat tethered beneath it as bait. But the night's vigil was in vain for the tiger did not turn up as expected. Still, we were most politely entertained to a stout breakfast in the morning. Villagers in India were most charming and hospitable, even though they were often near to starvation.

I remember playing cricket at a fashionable school on one occasion where we were served a most appetizing meal of several moist curries. Unfortunately, it was eaten in the traditional Indian way using bare fingers and pieces of chapatti torn off and used like a spoon. Not having the skill, practice, or indeed the prehensile fingers of the average Indian, we consumed an awful lot of chapatti in the process. While it says something about the quite unfamiliar meal I remember, I have forgotten who won the cricket match.

To commemorate the Day of Independence a military parade was held on 15 August 1947 at the Maidan Recreation Ground, Bombay. The following extract appeared in the *Bath Chronicle*:

Suddenly the pace of the music changed, a fanfare of bugles setting 180 paces to the minute for the 1st Battalion Somerset Light Infantry, represented by three full-strength companies and bearing their Regimental Colours. In olive green shirts and shorts, with green berets, stockings and hose-tops, they 'carried' the parade, absolutely the picture of precision and smartness – the only British troops on the parade.

They certainly deserved the applause they got and we felt especially proud since it was the good old Somerset Light Infantry who represented the British Forces in this particular parade. Even the Gurkha soldiers who followed, soldiers who have the highest respect for their bearing and smartness, were unable to put on a better show than the Somersets.

I was commanding the leading company. There had been a rumour that some violence might be directed against us and the police were anxious we should be driven back to barracks. However, our CO directed that we should march the couple of miles back to Colaba Point with one man in every three having his rifle loaded, not with a round in the breech, but ready for action within a second or so.

The exit from Maidan was too narrow for three ranks to pass abreast. There was some inevitable bunching and I was anxious about the obvious threat to us from Indian spectators crowding the balconies of a six-storey block of flats immediately above us. A couple of hand grenades tossed down from above would have been a disaster. My fears were unfounded – there was loud applause.

Ron Millward
RASC

There was no sweating troopship for me; we came out by air to Karachi, stopping at Rheims (France), Castel Benito (Tripoli), Lydda (Palestine) and Sha'bah (Iraq). Then we flew to Poona so it was only there, where we entrained for Secunderabad, that I saw the abject poverty and suffering that defies description. There were beggars of all descriptions – some with amputated or distorted limbs, others victims of elephantiasis, leprosy and many other diseases, and all crying out for 'baksheesh'.

Leaving Secunderabad for the three-day trip by rail to Bengal I learned my first valuable lesson. I entrusted my last rupee to a fruit vendor while leaning out of the carriage window. The train moved off and my remaining rupee stayed with him! Our destination was a place called – I think – Kankinara, on the banks of the wide Hoogli River near Calcutta. A place so humid that you sweated even when taking a shower. Prickly heat, dysentery, malaria, foot rot and ringworm were just a few of the many diseases we encountered. One notable cure, handed down from the regular soldiers who had served in India long ago, was to rub a raw onion on the affected sore. As ration sergeant I was referred to as the 'dispensing chemist' – much sought after and often running out of onions.

Once a week we were subjected to 'K' rations so there were no raw onions on that day. Incidentally, even today, I have recurrences of a particular problem which my doctor calls 'dhobi-wallah's itch'.

My duties involved a daily visit to the US airbase at Barrackpore. I once joined in a darts match there – Britain versus America. On their team was Jackie Coogan the American film star.

When supplying rations to Indian troops I recall they had to have their meat provided 'on the hoof'. I used to pick up about a dozen goats and take them to the unit for slaughter. Their butchers would put the goat's head through a hole in a wooden device and chop it off with just one blow of a sword. 'Halal' meat it was called. Different religions meant different customs.

There was a cholera epidemic when we were there and a total ban on drinking local mineral water. But we had whisky at only eight rupees a bottle and believed that cholera germs could not survive that.

Not only were germs a danger, so were sharks. Shark nets were used when we swam off the beautiful stretch of coast known as Elliott's Beach in Madras. It was here that some British ladies – bless them – used to serve things like salad teas at the Salvation Army canteen. You have no idea how good it was to have food prepared just as it would have been back in England.

Snakes were always a problem, of course, and once during a monsoon period there were suddenly thousands of tiny frogs jumping around everywhere. It was quite impossible not to tread on them.

Calcutta was a city crammed with human beings, roaming sacred cattle and dilapidated vehicles – the noise was incredible.

We left Bombay in 1947 to a certain amount of booing and hissing – not to mention the stone throwing, but it did not seem that there was any real hostility towards us. From a commercial point of view the ordinary Indian would soon be worse off.

Ken Flint
ROYAL SIGNALS

I recall the time we did a Command and Signals exercise during the monsoon season at Bilaspur. It was one of those schemes when only small groups go out to represent whole companies or batteries in the field.

Half a dozen of us were dropped off in the jungle to take the part of a complete battery. We had a radio, of course, and our personal sleeping gear but no tents because we were simulating having just been landed. To carry this gear we had the standard airborne cart, a two-wheeled flimsy affair nicknamed a 'pram' but in reality a light trolley rather like the trek carts boy scouts used to pull.

In charge was a sergeant from Regimental HQ. He was one of those know–it–all types, the kind of bloke who will never be told and always thinks he knows better than anyone else. He had only recently joined the unit and was not long out from Blighty, where he had been a bombardier in a training unit. Big and with flashing eyes, he used to strut and swagger instead of walking around like a normal ordinary mortal.

Our main task was to get the radio station set up and working so we could contact HQ. Having pushed the cart a few hundred yards along the narrow track with 'Sergeant Burra-Sahib' going ahead to find a suitable site, we were suddenly ordered to halt and off-load our gear.

The sergeant indicated we should set up our little HQ in the dry bed of a watercourse. We asked if this was wise because the monsoon had by no means finished and the watercourse might suddenly turn into a flowing stream. Also, if we stayed at the edge of the jungle we could tie a stone to a length of copper wire, fling it over the branches of a tree and so have a good aerial that would definitely get our signals back to camp. 'No,' he said, 'these sets are quite powerful and will easily get us through to RHQ if we put up an ordinary rod aerial because we are clear of the trees and our transmission will not be screened.'

'To our amazement the rod aerial worked quite well and we obtained strength 5 signals back at camp.'

I was one of the radio ops and so was my 'oppo'. Both of us were Royal Signals trained and experienced from service in north-western Europe. But 'orders is orders', as they say, so we followed the sergeant's orders. To our amazement the rod aerial worked quite well and we obtained strength 5 signals back to camp. 'There you are', said Sergeant Know-it-all triumphantly, 'I told you I was pretty good with wireless communications'. He then gave orders for the set to be manned by one of us while the rest gathered what dry wood they could find to make a fire. 'To keep jungle wildlife at bay!' he informed us.

So in no time at all we had a nice fire going, kindled by plenty of nice dry message forms, and managed to cook a good stew and brew some char. Meanwhile, messages were going back and forth and everything seemed to be OK. Pleased with the way things were running our 'boss' announced he was going to make a little 'bivvy' with his groundsheet and get some kip. So he wrapped himself up in his monsoon cape and spread his mozzy net over himself, first removing his boots and webbing. Darkness fell suddenly as it usually does in the tropics and with it a light preliminary shower of rain. I was operating the wireless set so flung my groundsheet and monsoon cape over our little cart and stood close to it with my head beneath the canopy. Predictable as ever, the rain increased and the dry stream bed slowly turned into a running river. My back and legs were comparatively dry and protected and I had the tiny wireless operator's lamp to read by. The sergeant, however, soon found himself actually lying in water. Bootless and in the dark, he began to thresh around to gather up all his gear. Barefoot he made for the bank, where he found the other four of the team fully clothed and booted reclining against tree trunks and protected from the worst of the pouring rain by their capes, groundsheets and the foliage.

The sergeant was drenched to the skin with his bare feet covered in mud. His foul temper did not improve things at all. Returning to the area he had selected to sleep, he eventually found his boots but took more than an hour to get them on. It rained pretty well all night. In the morning, at first light, he gave instructions to send a message back to HQ to say we were in a bad way. Within an hour it was a bright, hot day and we soon dried out. After standing around eating a cold breakfast washed down with mango juice, we received the news that the exercise had been abandoned.

We were picked up by one of our own officers who refused to allow the muddy and somewhat dishevelled sergeant into the cab of the truck. As if by magic, the officer produced a bottle of rum, informing us, 'The MO has authorized this'. We produced our piallas in double-quick time. The sergeant, in some disgrace, refused the rum, and was heard muttering about not drinking on duty.

Late in 1946 I applied for a two months' education course at Simla and soon found myself arriving with others at Kalka station on a local train from the main line at Ambala in the Punjab. Here we changed into our serge uniform for the cold journey up into the foothills of the Himalayas. We rode in a toy-like train on an extremely narrow-gauge line that wound for more than 50 miles through many tunnels and over many bridges. The line wound back on itself, making very slow progress through rocks and pine trees and it grew so cold we stopped wondering at this feat of engineering and huddled together in our greatcoats. Some complained of light-headedness in the rarefied air but most of us had been used to this sensation in the mountains of Baluchistan.

Because there were no motor cars in Simla we were obliged to walk from the station to our billet, which was in fact a large house built almost like an alpine lodge. The change in conditions of everyday life as we knew it was equivalent to being on another planet. There were no more mosquito nets to use, real beds instead of crude charpoys, ensuite bathrooms and, best of all, a dining-room just downstairs with bearers to wait on us at the table.

The next day we scrambled up narrow paths to the Viceregal Lodge, where the Viceroy and his staff would stay during the hot season on the plains below.

'We rode in a toy-like train on an extremely narrow-gauge line that wound for more than 50 miles through many tunnels and over many bridges.'

We assembled in the ballroom and Major Archie Wavell welcomed us with a short address. 'Simla was called by Kipling "Heaven's Gateway – full of angels and knights",' he said, and went on, 'but unfortunately you are here to work'.

So it was back to the classroom. Our teachers, NCOs of the Army Education Corps, were experts in their own field. They were soon able to communicate their enthusiasm for their own subject and the time went quickly. We lived like civilians, not like regimented soldiers, and in the evenings, after gentle homework or lounging around listening to All India Radio, we could take a stroll in the evening air. If we felt like it we could stroll down to the Birdwood Club, a little Other Rank's rendezvous where we could sit by a blazing coal fire, munch egg banjos and, instead of cold drinks, refresh the inner man with Indian-brewed stout.

Weekends were usually spent taking a leisurely walk into the straggling town of Simla where there were some shops and other civilized amenities. Notable among these were the Cecil Hotel and Davicos Restaurant. Major Wavell, like his father Field Marshal Wavell· and Viceroy, was of a poetic bent and one or two of us would try to write odd verses. Every year the Viceroy held an All India Poetry Competition and I was amazed to win a consolation prize of a few rupees.

Saturday afternoons and all day Sunday were free of guard duties, pickets, fatigues or any military chores. After tiffin most of us would saunter along the Mall in town, spruced-up soldiers obviously, but acting with an air of decorum, conscious of the high-class Indians and Europeans around. Even the hillmen down from districts bordering Tibet and Nepal walked with a jaunty equal-with-the-sahibs step. They were usually covered with trinkets of all kinds, their clothing was often dirty, yet they possessed that healthy look that stems from an open-air life and independence of mind. As a rule if we met Indian peasants on the plains we would avoid eye contact. But with these Mongolian-featured men and women with their slanted bold eyes, I would sometimes venture to exchange a grin. I sometimes felt too that if only they would have immersed themselves in a bath at our billet some of the younger women would have been fanciable.

There was a world of difference, however, when I used to fancy the best of the Parsee women while on leave in Bombay. Their opulent saris moving against their elegant figures in the cool breezes blowing off the ocean were simultaneously attractive and frustrating. The only feminine delights possible for the BORs were those in the out-of-bounds Grant Road area, where whores from the ages of ten to sixty hawked their dubious wares from tiny cell-like barred cribs. It was here, rumour had it, that the redcaps were reputed to give the erring squaddy time enough to be caught by them *in flagrante delicto* so that he could not get off the charge on a mere technicality. I recall three of us making this historic trip down Grant Road but we had the landau hood up and ventured quick glances at the wares on offer.

'I sometimes felt too that if only they would have immersed themselves in a bath at our billet some of the younger women would have been fanciable.' Ken Flint in the tub.

At the Davicos Restaurant in Simla they served afternoon teas with such delicacies as cream and jam, and muffins just oozing with butter, not to mention tea poured from proper pots into good china cups. But a soldier's habit dies hard and soon we would be in the Cecil Hotel standing at the bar, not to quench our thirsts because of the day's heat, but simply to act like licentious soldiery who are supposed to get drunk.

On one particular Saturday night there was a shemozzle in the upstairs cloakroom. Somebody had wrenched a large plate mirror off the wall and flung it into the Mall outside – not the sort of thing sahibs were supposed to do. Kipling would have understood because he sympathized with the lot of the poor British soldier in India. Unfortunately Kipling is dead, but one of the sergeant instructors was very much alive – and in the cloakroom at the time.

Attending to a call of nature I saw clearly the men who were perpetrating this act of vandalism. When the hotel manager complained to Archie Wavell next morning, the sergeant duly placed me on a 'fizzer'. One by one we came before Major Wavell. The guilty ones admitted their guilt, but I could only admit to being drunk and not to 'wilful destruction of civilian property'. Although pressed to name the ringleader, I declined. Unfortunately, I was the only one wearing a stripe. Such a charge against me might have been considered serious enough to warrant a court martial. Major Wavell had only the powers applicable

'Have you stuck to your promise, Corporal?' he enquired. 'Good man', he replied . . . We emptied our bladders in companionable silence . . .' Major Archie Wavell, second from right, at Simla. He was later killed in Kenya.

to a company commander. A court martial would have entailed sending me down to the plains and lamentably interrupting my course studies. So Archie compromised. He said he appreciated my refusing to name the ringleader, but since he felt I should suffer in some way he would sentence me to a sort of unofficial 'jankers'. I was not to visit Simla until the end of the course. I agreed, then I was subjected to a tongue lashing that left me trembling in fear. Until then I had looked upon him as a benevolent schoolmaster-type and quite removed from the fierce major he could be.

Archie used to conduct tutorials of an evening – more of a glass or two of sherry in his study and a discussion about one's career prospects. He gave a party at the Cecil to mark the end of the course. I remember climbing the stairs where both of us, probably light-headed, leaned against the bannister to catch our breath. Being slightly the worse for wear I said, 'Really, Sir, I should have checked with you that the course was finally over'. We had reached the landing before my remark sank in. I fancied he had forgotten I had been on house arrest. 'Have you stuck to your promise, Corporal?' he enquired. 'Good man', he replied when I said I had. We emptied our bladders in companionable silence and returned to the party.

Years later he was killed by the Mau Mau when the patrol he was leading was ambushed. A waste of a good man.

CHAPTER SEVEN

'The Night Sky Glowed Crimson'

India's twentieth and last Viceroy worked swiftly – too swiftly, some believed – towards partition. At the stroke of midnight on 14 August 1947 the Raj came to an end. Even as Lord Louis Mountbatten signed the official document, the flag that had flown day and night over the shell of the Residency at Lucknow ever since the 1857 mutiny, was finally lowered and the flag-pole removed.

But some British army units were still in the sub-continent, their position at times quite tenuous. They passed through regions which had never possessed any obvious political persuasion. Here and there the villages had changed little in a thousand years – masses of small mud huts, ill-lit, ill-ventilated, between them filthy little narrow unpaved streets on to which were thrown all the slops and refuse straight out of doors.

For many servicemen and women their visit to India or Burma was overshadowed by the burning sun, an unbearable climate, sickness and 101 other afflictions. The European was always vulnerable to such scourges as cholera and typhoid, as well as to such everyday irritants as dysentery and malaria, but they accepted this with remarkable equanimity.

And yet, no one – least of all the British serviceman – could go on living unassimilated in another's country and not be aware that they were, to a growing number of native inhabitants, unwelcome. The people had shown violence towards them in the past and had threatened at times to do so again. This, then, despite the pretensions of the Raj, was the shadow under which all the British in India especially lived their lives.

The July 1945 General Election back in Blighty resulted in an overwhelming defeat for the Conservatives at the hands of the Labour Party. This defeat sent shock waves through the British Empire but not the British serviceman.

Those under the age of twenty-one were not entitled to vote, those that were voted in the hope that a better and much fairer Britain would evolve. They held strong views that Conservatism meant wealth and privilege and authority for the few. The majority may have voted Labour but it is doubtful they were true

It was not beyond the ordinary soldier to recognize the beauty of the country, its buildings, its enormous variety of customs and cultures.

socialists. Their socialism was simply an expression of their desire not to return home to the dole queue, poor housing and abject poverty of which many had first-hand experience. They wanted jobs, security and a better education for their children. After all, it was what they had been fighting for, beyond the fact they were not prepared to let England become a satellite of the Axis powers.

And now they have their memories. In quieter moments, they can return to their regiments, battalions, companies and platoons. They can recall, in sharp focus, the images of poverty, starvation, disease and squalor in the sub-continent of India and the quaint semi-feudal culture of the sometimes beautiful land of Burma. With more intelligence than they were sometimes credited with, they knew it was impossible to attempt to westernize these peoples.

There is no doubt such sentiments existed. However, deep down in their subconscious there was that ever present feeling – although few will admit to it even now – of bewildered affection for the peoples of India. It was not beyond the ordinary soldier to recognize the beauty of the country, its buildings, its enormous variety of customs and cultures, the art forms and, not least, the magnificent Indian regiments decked out in their blazing ceremonial uniforms. They can remember, too, the smiling faces of little children begging for baksheesh, the clamour of humanity in the bazaar and the irrepressible spirit of the peoples who endured such unspeakable miseries, cruelties and poverty.

The 2nd Battalion Black Watch, led by pipers in full ceremonial dress, marched through Karachi with fixed bayonets and colours flying.

But time was running out for the British.

On 26 February 1948 the 2nd Battalion Black Watch paraded in Karachi and then embarked on the troopship *Empire Halladale*. The Royal Highland Regiment had first landed at Bombay in 1782 to fight the sepoys of the East India Company in the Mysore wars. They came for the fourth time in 1942 and took part in Orde Wingate's second Chindit expedition of 1944. Now they were to say farewell to Pakistan.

The battalion, led by pipers in full ceremonial dress, marched through the city of Karachi with fixed bayonets (a privilege specially accorded for the occasion) and colours flying, to parade in the grounds of Government House, for a royal salute to the Governor-General, Mr Jinnah.

Units of the Pakistan Army were assembled at the West Wharf, Keamari, and guards of honour of the 7th Baluchis and 2/16th Punjab Regiment had already formed up. The Black Watch formed three sides of a hollow square to hear a message from Mr Liaquat Ali Khan. The regimental colour dipped in salute to General Akbar Khan who addressed the troops. The King's colour and

The slow march of the 1st Battalion Somerset Light Infantry through the city of Bombay culminated at the Apollo Bundur, the scene in the past of the arrival and departure of successive viceroys and governors.

regimental colour were then slow-marched up the gangway of the *Empire Halladale* – the last British Army colours to leave Pakistan.

Two days later, India's farewell to the British Army on 28 February 1948 could not have been more impressive. The slow march of the 1st Battalion Somerset Light Infantry through the city of Bombay culminated at the Apollo Bundur, the scene in the past of the arrival and departure of successive viceroys and governors. There the last British troops in the Indian Dominion passed beneath the Gateway of India, the monumental structure erected to commemorate the visit of King George V and Queen Mary in 1911.

Before the march past the Governor of Bombay read to the departing troops messages from Earl Mountbatten, the Governor-General of India, and Pandit Nehru, the Prime Minister of the new dominion, and the final act was the embarkation of the colour party. Guards of honour were provided by units of the Royal Indian Navy and the Indian Army, including Mahrattas, Gurkhas and a detachment of Royal Sikhs in their red puggrees.

The Somersets boarded launches which took them out to the troopship *Empress of Australia* and away from a country which had been the scene of so many of their exploits.

What the war in the Far East created and achieved were a competent and trained Indian officer corps and a transfer of power within the framework of the well-established institutions. Perhaps these were Britain's most significant gifts to India.

Alan Chapman
10 SQUADRON TRANSPORT COMMAND

I had spent two years as ground crew on Halifaxes with Bomber Command and just after VE-Day converted to the Dakota aircraft flying out with the squadron to Bilaspur, Central Provinces. It was hardly a Garden of Oriental Delights for it was out in the wilds of India.

Soon after the war ended we started flying our released POWs from various pick-up points like Bangalore and Madras, taking them to Poona so they could be airlifted to Karachi and thence to Blighty. We called this particular job 'trooping', but it was really an errand of mercy. We must have flown two or three hundred of our released men, who were undernourished and sick, each day. But as they were going home their morale was pretty high. The accommodation at Poona, a long-established army base, was luxurious compared to what these men had previously known.

Early in 1946 we started another errand of mercy, dropping rice to the starving tribes on the Burma–China border. We lived in tents. I remember there

'. . . we started flying our released POWs from various pick-up points like Bangalore and Madras, taking them to Poona . . .' The loss of a Dakota of 10 Squadron at Poona.

was once a raging storm while we were watching a film at the open air cinema and the screen blew away into the jungle.

Back in Poona we were placed on red alert over the Indian Navy mutiny at Bombay. Three Dakotas were flown to Yellahanka to pick up rockets for a Typhoon squadron in case the balloon really went up. Then we moved to Karachi after the Indian Navy mutinied there, and there were several deaths from heat exhaustion as the temperatures exceeded 98 degrees Fahrenheit. I went home on the troopship HMS *Georgic*.

Ken Short
INDIAN AIRBORNE

In 1946 the regiment went off to do its first annual artillery range firing. At the time we were in Quetta. The site selected was Kalat, one of the many independent kingdoms in India. For much of the journey up to the Bolan Pass, which was equal in importance to the famous Khyber Pass, the roads were pukka – properly metalled. But once over the pass it was a case of bumpy tracks across wild and mountainous country. Our 15 cwt truck coped rather well but

'The men fastened up their bunks and either killed time on deck or else joined the endless, slow-moving queue to obtain a cup of tea . . .' The troopship HMS *Georgic*.

the many 3 tonners did not and the REME Light Aid Detachment made running repairs.

An advance party had gone on ahead. Our first job was to set up tents for the officers and a marquee for their mess. An officer soon enquired whether a sort of makeshift electric lighting system could be rigged up for the mess. We were a parachute unit and generators were not part of our gear. However, we did have small 'chore-horses' to make the current to charge our radio batteries.

We sited one of these well away from the mess and proceeded to lay the insulated cable. When we discovered there was not enough cable someone suggested making an overhead line. Necessity being the mother of invention, we scrounged 5 foot poles by divesting the officers' mess marquee of some of its supports. For insulators we used glass lemonade bottles fastened to the top of each pole and wound the copper wire round them.

In no time at all we had current to the mess, part underground and part overhead, the latter section less than 5 feet above ground. 'Excellent', our officer said. 'That's what I call a good bit of improvisation under field conditions. Let's hope nobody walks into the bare wires in the dark.' He walked out of his tent that same evening and was shocked in more ways than one. The news spread like wildfire.

Kalat State really consisted of thousands of miles of mainly rocky mountains and desert. We remained in this wilderness with not even the occasional camel to enliven the scene and our water was brought daily from an oasis by water bowsers.

The two-man detachment who maintained radio contact with Quetta about 60 miles away, had been there as part of the advance party. They had made a little sump in the desert where they poured all their washing water. Beside this was a tiny plot sprouting mustard and cress. One of the operators, making sure he had a regular supply of vitamins, had written to his parents back home for seeds. The seed packets had arrived by airmail in just one week!

During the day it was unbearably hot but at night it was as cold as the North Pole. Tea served with our evening meal was liberally laced with rum, which made conditions more tolerable.

Captain D.A.T. Thain
595 INDIAN AIRBORNE FIELD SECURITY SECTION

In early November 1946, 595 Indian Airborne Field Security Section had just completed one year's residence in Karachi, after its move from the remote jungle divisional assembly camp at Bilaspur in Central Provinces. Life in Karachi was pleasant and comfortable, but lazily so. Apart from the weekly exertions of the section's football team comprising BORs, IORs, an Indian cook and personnel borrowed from Divisional HQ Intelligence Branch, there was little or no physical exercise. The sergeant major and the FSO were both being overwhelmed by the ever-increasing flood of peace-time army forms and accounting documents. Consequently, it was decided to take advantage of the excellent weather of that time of year to run an all-embracing training camp for the section. The administrative arrangements took a couple of weeks to complete. The main preliminary tasks were the selection of a camping area and the assembly of all equipment considered necessary. Eventually, after a few recce flights in a Tiger Moth along the course of the Hub River near Karachi, the FSO decided on a spot where a clump of trees on the bank of the river overlooked a large stretch of water still remaining in the partly dried up river bed.

A general idea of the scope of training carried out the following week is given by the range of equipment taken out: 1,000 rounds of .303, 1,000 rounds of 9 mm, two 12-bore shotguns with 300 cartridges, 36 grenades, booby-trap equipment, two No. 22 signals sets, maps, marching compasses, medical equipment, two 180 lb tents with toggle ropes, water sterilizing equipment, sports kit, Pacific-type compo rations for one week for six British and eight Indian ranks, and last but by no means least, a couple of crates of beer. Personal equipment carried was limited to a bare minimum of battle order, arms and bedding roll.

A last minute recce by jeep was made on the ground and, this proving satisfactory, the section set out early next morning in one 3 ton truck and a jeep with trailer. The journey was less than 30 miles, but being across some difficult, almost trackless semi-desert country, it took nearly two hours. Within an hour of arrival the tents had been pitched, latrines dug, bedding lines for mosquito nets prepared and cooking facilities completed ready for lunch. The river bed at this point was sandy and rocky, about 150 yards wide, but the stream itself had dried up to a width of about 40 to 50 feet with a depth of about 6 feet.

On the first afternoon a few hand grenades were thrown into the stream to deter any crocodiles that might have been lurking there, and then stretches of water were clearly marked off for drinking purposes, swimming and washing. At about 1700 hrs the first duck appeared, flying upstream, and soon three had been bagged for the evening meal.

The normal routine was reveille at 0700 hrs, breakfast at 0745 hrs, first parade at 0830 hrs, and then a march to nearby cliffs for either small arms practice or map reading, returning to camp in time for lunch. In the afternoons radio procedure was practised, booby traps demonstrated, or fishing carried out with grenades and mosquito nets. The evenings were left free for games of soft-ball or a trek along the stream duck shooting. The No. 22 signals sets proved their entertainment value in the evenings when tuned in to All India Radio which was transmitted through the camp by loudspeakers constructed with headphones in biscuit tins.

The duck-shooting trek gradually developed into one of the most strenuous exercises of the day and, as the general school of thought was to get as close as possible to the birds on the water and then blast them at point-blank range, it proved to be an excellent test of fieldcraft, besides providing a welcome addition to the compo ration menu.

Our map reading schemes were planned to cover distances ranging from 7 miles on the first day to 15 miles on the seventh. This gradual build-up was necessary as two of the NCOs had broken their legs three months previously. On the third day, however, two of the NCOs, whose keenness exceeded their map reading ability, completed a cross-country march of nearly 20 miles. All training was carried out on a competitive basis by pairs of NCOs, each pair consisting of one British and one Indian or Gurkha. By this means a close understanding and spirit of comradeship was maintained and interest was kept up throughout the week. Outdoor life provided a welcome break from the routine work in Karachi – appetites developed, muscles toughened and everyone felt fighting fit.

The atmosphere by the river was delightfully fresh in the mornings and evenings, and really warm for sunbathing or swimming in the afternoons. Duck and pigeon shooting was tried by everyone, and a few odd rounds were successfully expended on jackals caught in the jeep headlights at night. Dress was left fairly free and easy, the main stipulation being that personnel did not allow themselves to get blistered by the sun or by battle order rubbing on bare skin. The resulting variety of dress, combined with the oddities of the jungle hat, made the section look rather like some irregular native levy. One of the trophies of the CSM was a snapshot of the FSO bending over a camp fire wearing only a bush-shirt.

As a climax to the week's camping, the whole section, less the CSM who drove the jeep and trailer, marched back in pairs across country carrying arms and battle order. It covered about 18 miles over barren, rocky and hilly terrain. The pairs set out at five minute intervals with instructions to find their own way home. Everyone made it with creditable performances, particularly considering the two NCOs who had left hospital in September with broken legs. The very healthy reaction of the section meant they had not degenerated into 'chairborne' troops.

Philip James
33 FIELD SQUADRON ENGINEERS

First raised as King George Vs Own Bengal Sappers and Miners, by 1943 we were part of the 44th Division, when that formation was armoured. It converted to airborne about December 1944. We moved to a jungle training area at Bilaspur early in 1945, preparing for a series of operations that were called off just before the atom bombs were dropped on Japan. We thought we might be wanted for Operation 'Zipper' (landings in Malaya), or a landing in Indo-China, but off we went to the mountains of Baluchistan. Most of my sepoys were Pushtu-speaking Pathans and were quite at home in that sort of terrain.

After completing a parachute demonstration jump at Roorkee, we were sent to the Punjab to recce possible sites for Dakota and light aircraft landing strips.

When the Punjab Boundary Force was formed it was pretty certain the Punjab would be divided and trouble would result. In July 1947, and being used mainly in an infantry role, we arrived in Amritsar as the only Muslim unit wearing red berets. Soon we became the targets for sniping and mortar fire from both army and police deserters. They were well armed and organized in groups with plenty of ammunition. At times, in support of our 'gangbuster' operations, we used light aircraft for observation and a half-troop of armoured cars. Our main commitment was guarding thousands of Muslim refugees crammed into

Amritsar railway station en route to safety in Pakistan. Both my second-in-command and another officer on loan from 40 Airborne Squadron Engineers, were killed in the city trying to protect and evacuate Muslim refugees.

Our men, Pathans and Punjabi Mussulmans, were all for going to war with India there and then. Lest we sought vengeance, General Pete Rees, a splendid man, in command of the Punjab Boundary Force, moved us into Pakistan.

The amazing thing is that in Pakistan we were used again in an infantry role. This time, after helping Sikh and Hindu refugees, we helped hold the line of the Ravi River against Indian attacks. We discovered that the Indian troops opposite us had been part of 50 Brigade Airborne Division before partition. Six months earlier we had been playing hockey against one another.

I cannot speak too highly of my Subedar Saif Ali MBE, who went on to become a major in the Pakistan Army. I went back to visit him eleven years later but in 1994, on a last visit to Pakistan we discovered he had died. However, my former batman Sapper Sawab Gul was alive and well and his family gave us a great welcome.

Matt Nash
2ND BATTALION BLACK WATCH

Hopes of a peaceful existence in the North West Frontier Province gradually lessened during the last few weeks of the battalion's stay in Peshawar. It was with some misgivings as to how long it would be before we saw them again that the rear party watched the train carrying the last half of the battalion steam out of the cantonment station. The rear party consisted of six officers and some sixty 'Jocks'.

As soon as the battalion had gone the business of handing over the barracks began, and at the same time we started to arrange our journey to Karachi. The date fixed for our departure was 20 August 1947, about a week after the battalion had departed. But conditions along the railway line after 15 August, the day of the transfer of power, rapidly deteriorated, until, after our departure had been postponed three times, the day came when we were told that there was no hope of us leaving in the foreseeable future! We were, in fact, almost completely cut off. There were no trains running at all, and the only communication was by air since the roads were also unsafe.

We sent numerous signals to the battalion asking for an air-lift. The refugee problem, however, was keeping the RAF fully occupied. After the hand-over was completed – a process which dragged on interminably as the MES employees were Sikhs or Hindus, and far more interested in preserving their own skins – the rear party settled down for a long wait. Guards were provided for all barrack blocks and stores, as there had been several cases of theft, and we could not take any risks regarding our arms. Morale was good – surprisingly so, since we had not received any mail once the main battalion had left.

All seemed normal until Sunday 7 September. At about 0930 hrs a fusillade was heard, and thereafter a certain amount of intermittent firing. Major Irwin went at once from the mess to the barrack block and ordered all men inside to ensure that no one should get involved in any incident. Extra guards were posted at once. He then visited the orderly room of the 3/8 Punjab Regiment (Muslims), who had moved into the other half of the barracks a week or so before. There he learned that a patrol of the 3/8 Punjab and a patrol of the 19th Lancers (Sikhs and Hindus), had clashed; two Punjabs had been killed and several Lancers wounded.

No more trouble was expected. But news travelled fast. By 1200 hrs some two thousand tribesmen and villagers had collected outside the cantonment. The whole rear party was reminded once again that we were strictly forbidden to take part in any of the troubles, unless, of course, we ourselves were actually threatened. Firing recommenced at about 1230 hrs and half an hour later the cantonment was swarming with tribesmen in lorries, tongas and on foot, intent on the murder of all Sikhs (in particular), and all Hindus (as a sideline), and the looting of shops owned by them.

Having overseen all the necessary precautions, our officers returned by various covered routes to the mess, over which bullets were fired almost continuously. The meal, and those over the next three days, was consumed with a loaded revolver ready to hand.

During the afternoon, more tribesmen entered the city and by evening the Sikh quarter was burning furiously. The whole of the night sky glowed crimson. The authorities considered that it would never be known how many had perished in the flames, for we were told that tribesmen not only surrounded the burning area, preventing anyone leaving, but they actually drove people from other quarters into the conflagration!

On Monday morning Major Irwin was called to help with the refugee problem. The command of the rear party fell upon Captain Lindsay. Before long six tonga-loads of tribesmen galloped up the road through the barracks and attacked the canteen (owned by a Hindu). Although they did considerable damage they failed to find the Hindu staff, most of whom were concealed in barrels in the cellar. Looting continued unabated during the day along the Mall and in the Saddar Bazaar area. By this time nearly all Sikhs and Hindus who had not been murdered were concentrated in various large buildings – but they were only safe temporarily.

The canteen manager, disguised as a Muslim, decided on Tuesday to make for safety in a building in the Saddar Bazaar. He got as far as the gate of the officers' mess, where a passing band of tribesmen recognized him. He was shot seven times and finally killed with a meat cleaver. This sort of thing went on until Wednesday afternoon, by which time the military and police were organized and speedily drove the tribesmen off. Isolated incidents, however, continued all over the cantonment and the city and presented a dismal spectacle. All Hindu shops had been attacked and looted, bodies lay about, and scattered parties were still to be seen intent on looting.

On Friday 12 September we received a signal from the battalion that one Dakota would arrive at Peshawar the following day to bring away certain personnel who were urgently needed in Karachi. We were ordered to the airfield but the aircraft had broken down at Chaklala. The next day and on subsequent days we waited – in vain. The plane finally appeared on the Monday and arrived at Mauripur at 2230hrs after an uneventful flight. Lieutenants Carver, Russel-Cargill and Bridger and the MO and about forty men remained behind. They were to fly down a few days later. When four Dakotas arrived to pick them up the 'Jocks' had already left by train.

The battalion's first few weeks in Malir were, naturally enough, spent settling into the new camp. The camp had previously been occupied by Indian troops who had pursued a 'scorched earth' policy before handing over to us. In the space of a few days, however, the orderly room was smartened up, as were the company lines, and the whole resembled the smooth flower beds and sweeping drives associated with a Government House, instead of an ugly, open patch of dry desert.

After the heat and minor ills of Peshawar, many men decided to take a spot of local leave. Sanspit was the most popular destination, and there was little to do out there except laze in the sun and swim, but there was a YMCA. Other men preferred to spend their leave nearer the fleshpots of Karachi, and so stayed at the Karachi YMCA or at the excellent Union Jack Club.

In the middle of September, when the flare-up at Delhi was at its height, the battalion was ordered to carry out air transport training. Everything had to be ready in forty-eight hours and, as you can imagine, a vast amount of work was done. Two Dakota mock-ups were made available to practise drills in emplaning and deplaning, but as the trouble in Delhi dried out, the training fizzled out also.

On 25 September we heard that the Supreme Commander, Field-Marshal Auchinleck, was to visit the battalion the very next day. He arrived on the square at 0800hrs to find the battalion drawn up in line, with the colour party in the centre and the flag staff and saluting base already waiting. The RSM and the Pioneers must have worked overnight. The effect was excellent, even though the Field-Marshal's shoes did lift some of the wet paint from the steps as he mounted the platform!

Within a few months four age and service groups had left the battalion, and one consolation was that British troops in Pakistan were now sailing from Karachi, which saved them the ghastly journey round to Bombay, and the long wait in the Homeward Bound Trooping Depot. A fair percentage of the battalion always succeeded in getting down to the docks to see the ships off. Perhaps the best farewell was given to 60 and 61 Groups. These were the largest single batch of men ever to leave the battalion – one officer and 130 men. Our pipes and drums played on the quayside alternatively with those of the Royal Scots. Field-Marshal Sir Claude Auchinleck spoke a few words to those on board, and as the ship pulled out, the pipes and drums played 'How Happy We Have Been A'together', breaking into 'Heilan' Laddie' as she got further out into the stream.

When on 27 October the 14th Field Regiment Royal Artillery, left for home, they bequeathed us their transport. We took them down to the ship and our pipes and drums played them away. There seemed every chance that we might have to ferry ourselves to the docks, the last vehicles being left on the quayside!

Our move from Pakistan was still a matter of conjecture. Just a week or two back plans had been firm for us to embark in the *Empress of Australia* on Christmas Eve. Since then, however, it was realized that British families would still be passing through Karachi at the beginning of January 1948. It was considered necessary to have a British battalion there until everyone was clear.

The new reorganization of the British Army demanded that the 2nd Battalion Black Watch be reduced to cadre form. The blow was indescribable. We were living very much in the present and dare not think too deeply of what the future holds in store. News has been received that on our arrival home we will probably go to a camp at Comrie. There, presumably, the battalion will spend the last days of its 170 years of unbroken service.

Epilogue

'Wapas jao', I seem to remember, was crude Urdu for 'go back', and Major Stanley Hamilton MBE, actually went back in November 1992. This is what he said about that return journey:

I wrote to Brigadier Chand SM VSM, of the 50th Indian Parachute Brigade at Agra, and he said he would be delighted to welcome me. I was late arriving in Agra and where a Major Patil had been trying to contact me. You can imagine my pleasure when I found he was the OC of 622 ASC Para. the direct descendant of my old RIASC Company.

I was invited to visit them and told that transport would be sent. Sharp on time a highly polished Russian-made jeep drew up at my hotel complete with a lieutenant as aide. My prestige went up in the eyes of the Pathan doorman and from then on when I went in and out I was given pukka salutes. On arrival at the company lines I was greeted formally but warmly by the OC's 2nd IC and senior warrant officer standing rigidly to attention. We then repaired out of the bright sun to a shaded area for me to meet the officers and NCOs over an informal tea.

They were a complete mixture of religions and were bound only by loyalty to their unit, the red beret and para wings. Since Independence many of them had seen active service – obviously mostly against Pakistan and China, although officially they were not allowed to say so. Many had been decorated for gallantry.

I was the first British officer of the company from which theirs was a direct descendant who had ever returned and they seized on me with great interest, especially as I had some vintage photographs of parachuting in the old days. Copies were taken for their unit archives.

Major Patil had thoughtfully invited a contemporary [of mine], Lieutenant Colonel T.G.N. Pai VRC, with his wife and grandchild. Colonel Pai had commanded 622 Company on two occasions and we had plenty of notes to compare.

After a visit to tea with the deputy brigade commander – such hospitality overwhelmed me – the OC of 622 drove me back to my hotel where I was greeted with "burra salaams" from the Pathan doorkeepers. It had been the highlight of my visit. The Taj Mahal was fine, the sights and sounds of Delhi, Agra and Jaipur were thought-provoking, but my visit to 622 Coy ASC of the 50th Indian Parachute Brigade, Indian Army, will stay with me for the rest of my days.

THE KOHIMA MEMORIAL

After the Japanese were driven out of Kohima, numerous infantry battalions of the 2nd Division erected their own memorials to the many areas where fierce battles had taken place. Some of these were situated on remote hilltops in the surrounding countryside.

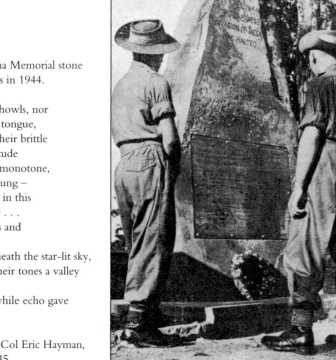

The original Kohima Memorial stone set in the Naga Hills in 1944.

'Silence. No jackal howls, nor
    distant gun gives tongue,
The crickets cease their brittle
    morse: The quietude
Seems as a chanted monotone,
    not heard – not sung –
Yet present, woven in this
    pregnant solitude . . .
The misted chaungs and
    lofty, noble trees
Lie still and silent 'neath the star-lit sky,
And then, as bells their tones a valley
    fills,
I heard his Voice, while echo gave
    reply.'

From A Trilogy by Col Eric Hayman,
4 (WA) Brigade 1945.

The 2nd Division, after pursuing the remnants of the Japanese into Tamu and Palel and on to the Chindwin River, then encamped along the Kohima–Imphal Road to rebuild their losses and prepare for the next move over the Chindwin.

While there plans were laid to build a divisional war memorial beside the cemetery at Kohima. Near Maram, on Milestone 80, were a number of obelisk stones which had been erected to Naga chieftains in bygone days. Permission had been granted for one of these huge headstones to be dug out to provide the main headstone for the proposed memorial. The stone obelisk lay about 1 mile from the main road with a very steep upward slope leading to its resting place. A road was cut in a zig-zag fashion by a bulldozer which enabled a huge Scammel transporter, equipped with winch and crane, to negotiate the steep hill. Without the Scammel the stone, approximately 16 feet long, 3 feet wide and about 18 inches thick, would have tumbled down a ravine, of which there were several.

Eventually, the 17 ton stone reached the Kohima road where a tank transporter was waiting. An appropriate area was then chosen adjacent to the road and the headstone was lifted off at the foot of Garrison Hill. The cooperation between the REs and RAOC had enabled the stone to be moved, but now it was the turn of the Naga tribesmen. A Naga chieftain and his tribesman pushed, pulled and generally manhandled the headstone into position, with no more equipment than strong ropes, pulleys and sandbags. The whole operation took several hours to complete until, after much singing and chanting, the stone dropped into its final resting place.

Had the task been left to the sappers (as one recalled many years afterwards), it would probably have ended up being recognized as a great feat of military engineering. The stone now stands as the great headstone of the 2nd Division Memorial surrounded by the graves of many servicemen who had fought and died at Kohima in 1944. The fitting epitaph engraved upon it has become widely known and is often quoted at Remembrance Day services.

'WHEN YOU GO HOME, TELL THEM OF US AND SAY,
FOR YOUR TOMORROW, WE GAVE OUR TODAY.'

On a purely historical note, the correct wording for the Kohima Memorial should have been: 'WHEN YOU GO HOME, TELL THEM OF US, AND SAY, FOR YOUR TOMORROWS, THESE GAVE THEIR TODAY.' The words have been attributed to J.M. Edmunds, a classics scholar and one-time Master at King's School, Canterbury. An amended plaque was erected in 1963.

SO SOON

Have you so soon shut tight
The door
And drawn the curtain?
The sun is bright
Above the heather on the moor.
Have you so soon let die
The fire
And put the book down?
The woods are shy
And dark with Autumn's gold attire.
Have you so soon turned down
The light
And gone to sleep?
The leaves are brown
And brittle on the road tonight.
Ay, draw the curtains, bolt the door
Upon the past;
But while you sleep
The shining arrows that we cast
Return to keep alive the careless days
(The wild, free reckless days!)
And stabbing deep,
Bring images that seem
More real than any dream.

P.J. Martin
April 1945

Appendix I

MAP OF INDIA & BURMA - showing the principal areas of SEAC COMMAND and its insignia.

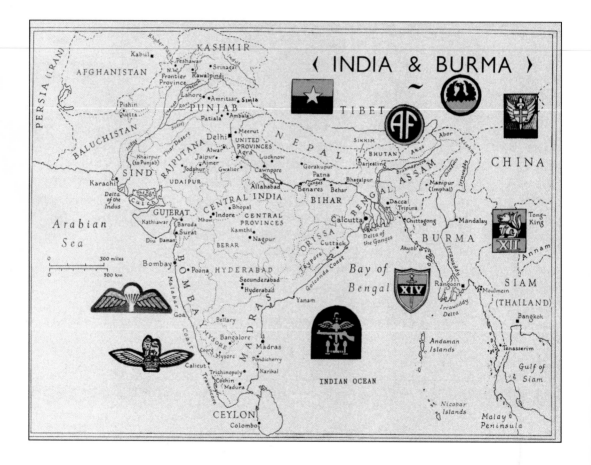

Appendix II

MAP OF BURMA - *showing the principal insignia of ARMIES, CORPS and DIVISIONS used during the Burma campaigns.*

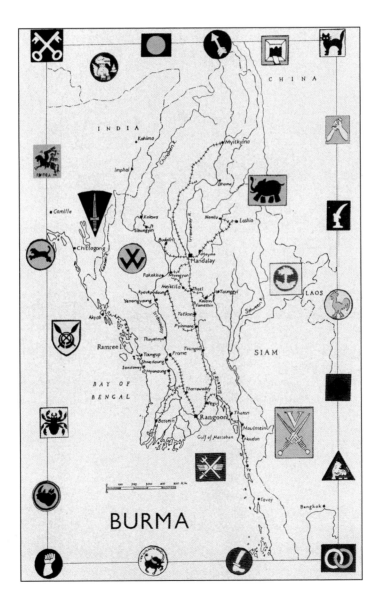

Index